The People's 1

Newbiggin b

by

Mike Kirkup

This majestic building known as the Bank House was eventually turned into a workingmen's club in 1901.

Previous page: Pleasure boats on Newbiggin beach in the 1930s.

Copyright © Mike Kirkup 2002

First published in 2002 by

The People's History Ltd
Suite 1 Byron House
Seaham Grange Business Park
Seaham
Co. Durham
SR7 0PY

ISBN 1 902527 86 0

Contents

Acknowledgements 4

Introduction 5

1. Perils of the Sea 7

2. Flotsam … 19

3. 'The New Era' 35

4. Sandshoe Days 47

5. Co-operation and Coalmining 59

6. … and Jetsam 69

7. 'Alaang the Narra Path' 83

8. Newbiggin Dates (Faces and Places) 107

Acknowledgements

Much praise is due to other writers who have documented a great deal of information in previous books on Newbiggin, such as Bill Harrison, John Lisle Robinson, Bill Ogilvie, Tom Chape and Richard Martin whose recent publication *150 Years of Newbiggin Lifeboat House* will reward the reader with a rare insight into the heroism of brave locals who risked their lives for others. Help with information and photos was also given by Tom and Edna Armstrong, John Talbot, Colin Wanless, Betty Carter, Gordon Burn, Bill Harris, Tom Johnson, Sheila Bound, Brian Lupton, Peggy Punton and the families of the late George Nesbit and Jack and Jim Adams. The sensitive illustrations were provided by Vera Hook and Alan Ross, while the cartoons were skilfully drawn by Les Davison, the late Ron Herdman of the *Ashington Advertiser*, plus Will Robson, J. Short and D. Yarrow from the 1920's team of illustrators with the *Ashington Colliery Magazine*.

Thanks also to Ross Weeks of the *News Post Leader* and Vince Gledhill of the *Newcastle Evening Chronicle* for passing on newspaper articles from the past; also the *Herald & Post* for their ongoing support. And thanks are due to the countless people, such as J.V. Hughes, Cush Todd, Jean Stacey, Jack Hodgetts, Peter Robinson, Eric Dodds, Edie Lockyer, Ray Wear, John White, Rose Hails, Margaret Norman, Eric Nichol, Noreen McMahon, Dorothy Harold, Doreen Kailofer and Lucille Charlton plus many others, who have provided their memories and photos depicting what it was like to be either a Newbiggin resident or simply a day-visitor to this charming seaside town.

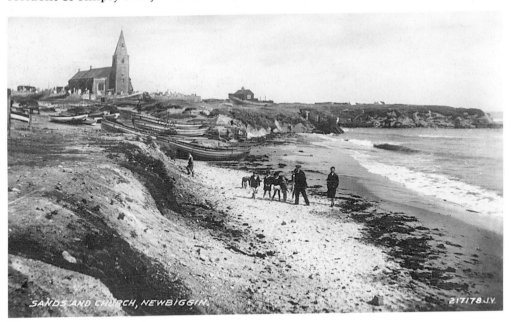

SANDS AND CHURCH, NEWBIGGIN.   217178 J.Y.

Back cover: In the mid-1990s, Northumberland County Council ran a 'Healthy Eating' campaign in local schools. Jack Thompson, who was then Wansbeck's MP, was on hand at Newbiggin's Moorside First School to sample the nutritious menu with the dinner ladies and some of the children. Dinner ladies from left: Joan Martin, the late Joyce Milburn, Joyce Rutter, Jean Harrison and Louvaine Robinson. Children: Leigh Milne, Alan Thain, Sharna Middleton, Geoffrey Robson, Amy Smith and Holly Sutherland.

Introduction

There is no more welcoming sight these days than Newbiggin by the Sea with some summer sunshine on its back. The 21st century has seen the little village come of age, closing for all time the divide between the 'fisher-end' and the 'west-end' of the town. A hundred years ago the split was there for all to see, with the meagre fishermen's cottages lying almost in the sea, contrasting the villas and lodging houses standing haughtily above the Bay.

Newbiggin has a history which links up this district with kings and princes and old wars, and its roots go deep. The exact depth to which these roots have attained may never be accurately known. We shall examine the origins of how this strange blending of fishing village, colliery village and one-time holiday resort has grown.

Newbiggin was in the Parish of Woodhorn, and the church (seen here next to a windmill with sails intact), has a history that goes back about 800 years.

A description of Newbiggin in the early nineteenth century is given by Mackenzie in his 'History'. He records that the village of Newbiggin 'contained some tolerably good houses, with four inns and public houses, and several shops for the sale of necessary articles. It is much frequented in the summer season for the convenience of bathing. The population of Hirst is barely fifty while Newbiggin boasts 437 souls.'

Tomlinson in his *Guide to Northumberland* writes: 'Newbiggin was formerly a maritime town of some importance. In the Wars of Edward II with Scotland, 'Newbygging' was required to furnish a ship for naval purposes. Large quantities of corn used to be shipped at this port and vessels of many tons burden rode in the harbour.' A pier was built along the rocks at the north side of the bay – a sort of breakwater, formed of large masses of rock piles. It is said that portions of these piles were plainly visible at low water up to the middle of the eighteenth century, but there does not seem to be any record of when it was built or by whom. The Newbiggin of old had fishing cobles lying around all over the shoreline and a headland that stretched far into the distance.

During the whole of the 18th and well into the 19th century, Newbiggin did a good trade in the shipment of corn, as was also the case with regard to the River Wansbeck, near North Seaton. Many granaries were erected parallel to the beach at Newbiggin. Says one authority: 'Corn ships of 60-tons burden came to the town. These were kept in the deep water of the bay. Large ships could ride in five, six or seven fathoms of water, in absolute security from the tempests of the north and east.' (Note, a fathom is six feet.)

Newbiggin must have been a romantic place in those days, especially for children who would have revelled in the excitement of the arrival and departure of ships:

'I remember the black wharves and the slips,
And the sea tides tossing free;
And foreign sailors with bearded lips,
And the magic of the sea.'

Records as far back as 1240 show that Newbiggin and its township was 'held by John de Baliol whose third son became King of Scotland', and who gave his name, not only to Baliol (Balliol) College, but to the nursing home built here in Newbiggin in the 1990s. The ownership of Newbiggin underwent many changes. It was

Illustration from *Ashington Colliery Magazine.*

held by Lord Widdrington, 'a gallant gentleman of revolutionary sympathies', who interested himself in the Jacobite Rising, and allied himself to the Stuarts, who sought to depose George I in favour of James (the son of James II), better known as the 'Old Pretender'. Rebellion broke out in Scotand and the north of England, and Lord Widdrington, in the manner of the times, led his men into battle. No doubt he fought courageously in a lost cause, and when the

Fisherfolk drawn by Vera Hook.

revolutionaries were defeated, he was lucky to escape with his life, for many of his associates in the uprising were executed. However, he was found guilty of high treason and his estates (which included Newbiggin) were forfeited to the Crown.

A 1855 *Morpeth Herald* reported: 'While Newbiggin may be superficially changing in response to the demands of an aggressive civilisation, there is one section of the community – the fisherfolk – which still wrestles a meagre and precarious livelihood from the changeless sea which rolls and surges, majestic in comparison to the long littleness of human life. Their work is essentially hazardous, hard and grim. Newbiggin Village was probably founded by fisherfolk who must have launched their vessels into the darkness centuries ago. Theirs has been a patient struggle in defiance to the threat of the sea which holds for them all the possibility of tragedy.'

SECTION ONE

PERILS OF THE SEA

Needle's Eye Rocks, Newbiggin. 11354.

It is impossible to say with certainty how many ships have come to grief around the shores of Newbiggin, but the Needle's Eye Rocks seen above claimed their fair share. Yet it was always a favourite haunt for youngsters who dared each other as to who could venture farthest out.

The 19th century opened disastrously for Newbiggin. On 14th January 1801, the crew of five fishing boats belonging to Newbiggin, Blyth and Hartley, perished at sea in a such violent and unexpected storm, they disappeared in 'the heave and halt, the hurl and crash of the comber wind-hounded sea.' No less than ninety persons were deprived of bread-winners. A public subscription was quickly organised which reached £1,701 for widows, orphans and dependants.

Newbiggin suffered a tragedy on 18th March 1851, with the loss of ten fishermen. Five colleagues valiantly attempted to save four crews of capsized cobles and they manned a coble for that purpose and managed to save two men. There was a realisation that more than a five-man coble was needed if lives were to be saved. Local action was successful in efforts to establish a Lifeboat Station. Rear Admiral His Grace the Duke of Northumberland accepted the office of President of the RNLI and contributed 100 guineas to general funds as well as undertaking to complete the coast of Northumberland with Lifeboats, including one for Newbiggin, all at his own expense. On 1st June 1851, five of the rescuing fishermen were awarded the Institute's Silver Medal. They were John Dent, Henry Brown, Philip Jefferson and William and Robert Armstrong.

NEWBIGGIN BY THE SEA LIFEBOAT.

Newbiggin Lifeboat House has retained its original facade over the entrance for 150 years. Richard Martin's evocative book *150 Years of Newbiggin Lifeboat*, again tells us that the *Newcastle Journal* carried this report on 11th October 1851: 'The foundation stone of a Lifeboat House was laid a few days ago at Newbiggin on which the health of the Duke of Northumberland ... was drunk with great enthusiasm. An address to the Noble Duke expressive of the gratitude for the munificent gift of a Lifeboat for the district is in the course of preparation.'

A year later, on 9th October 1852, a Newcastle newspaper reported: 'On Wednesday this week a trial of the self-righting powers of the new Lifeboat for Newbiggin ... took place in Shields Harbour ... the Lifeboat is waiting for placement at Newbiggin once the weather is sufficiently favourable.'

A week later: 'On Monday 11th October 1852 the splendid new Lifeboat for Newbiggin was delivered … on reaching the shore, the boat was immediately hauled up to the House … the hardy fishermen finished off with several rounds of hearty cheers for their great benefactor, the Noble Duke.'

Less than a month later, the new Lifeboat, named *Latimer* (after one of the eight Baronees of the House of Percy), with 'Big' Philip Jefferson as it first coxswain, was launched in a rescue bid, saving the lives of 'several fishermen of Newbiggin who, in their cobles, had been surprised by a gale which suddenly sprung up on 13th November 1852'.

At one minute the sea around Newbiggin can be as calm as a mill pond and the next it can dash to pieces even the strongest boats. The photos show how invaluable were the services of women in launching and housing the Lifeboat.

'Will the Grace Darlings of Newbiggin man the Lifeboat?'

That was the speculative headline in the *Morpeth Herald* on 12th December 1857. Grace Darling, a lighthouse-keeper's daughter, had earlier distinguished herself by rowing out to rescue men aboard the *Forfarshire* when she floundered off the Farne Islands. The *Herald* went on:

'The Newbiggin Lifeboat was launched recently when her qualities were well displayed in a rough sea entering Cambois River … the boat is highly appreciated by the fishermen, and suggestions have been made for forming a crew of females in case of emergency when their sweethearts and relatives are off, engaged in their vocation. Surely Grace Darlings will be found to step forward in so laudable a cause, for not infrequently, a woman's courage towers above her. We hope to give a list of such crew members in our next number.' Without the help of the women, such as in our previous photos, Newbiggin boats might never have left the shore.

It is to the well-being of 19th century Newbiggin residents on shore that we now look, via this Health Report delivered by Dr J.C. Reid in 1877: 'Before proceeding to review 1874, permit me to call the attention of the Board to a singular fact that, from 1844 to 1877, a period of over thirty years, there were only three women died in childbirth. Another observation is that the increase of deaths from debility or premature birth is greatly increased, as also abortions and miscarriages, nor has this been confined to the human species alone, both cows and mares, as their owners have experienced, have suffered in this neighbourhood during the last two years. I attribute this to atmospheric influence. I remarked the same thing 25 years ago, referring to the impurity and scarcity of water.

'There were, during the last quarter of a century (1850-75), few deaths from accident except on sea, still fewer from violence and only one man murdered, and that was generally thought a mistake and by strangers. I am not aware of a native of Newbiggin being tried and condemned at a Quarter Session or Assize Court and the great majority of police cases arise from the class of visitors which we would be better without. Suicide is of rare occurrence, no more than three in 25 years.' In photo we see here a 'better class of visitor'. Not a sign of violence on Newbiggin Beach in 1890. Although some ladies are hiding under parasols.

The *Morpeth Herald* reported in 1855 the existence of a well at Newbiggin, full of spring water, that was submerged every 24 hours, that 'retained its purity throughout the vicissitudes of time and tide.' The newspaper also reported: 'The low line of coast that stretches from the Church Point northwards and to a position to the eastern extremity of the Moor is where the well is located.'

Referring to a 1904 Health Report by Dr Burrow: 'Three cases of Smallpox in Newbiggin occurred, the first in Brewery Yard. The source of the infection was either from North Seaton or Hirst, or indirectly by a lot of second-hand clothing which was obtained from North Shields. The case was removed to Ashington Isolation Hospital (Pity Me) and the contacts in the house and adjoining two houses were barricaded in.' The photo above shows the 1926 ambulance used for the Pity Me Isolation Hospital at North Seaton.

According to Robert 'Cush' Todd's diary, 'at least three water pumps operated in the village: one beside Downie's butcher's shop in Woodhorn Lane; one beside the Railway Station; and one near the Cresswell Arms.' There were also a number of private wells serving individual houses. The fisherfolk used to get their water from the 'Pant', which was situated near the access road to the beach beside Attlee Cottages. Apparently, that one was 'done away with' when a new Sea Wall was built in 1960. Boys are seen here doing their ablutions at the popular East End Pump, not far from the Cresswell Arms.

On 22nd March 1900 there was a spectacular wreck, right on Newbiggin beach for all to see and examine. The schooner *Aspirant* had run ashore and the crew of six had been safely taken off by the Lifeboat. It is recorded that a local farmer, Septimus Grey, negotiated to buy the complete vessel and its furnishings, many of which ended up in his farmhouse.

The Northumberland Electric Tramways Act of 1902 was to empower the Northern Counties Electricity Supply Company to construct tramways and tramroads from Morpeth to Bedlington and Ashington, and then to Newbiggin.

The Ashington Tramway No 7 was to 'commence in the road from Bothal to Ashington ... at a point to the south-west corner of Woodbine Terrace and terminating at a point ... at Acacia Terrace.' Tramway 8 was 'wholly along a private road 6 furlongs and 5 chains in length in Ashington, Hirst and North Seaton, terminating by a junction with the road from Stakeford to Newbiggin.'

Tramway No 9 'is double situate in the townships of North Seaton and Newbiggin-by-the-Sea ... terminating at a point in High Street, Newbiggin, opposite the south-west corner of the King's Head.' Needless to say, none of the above ventures came to fruition, but what an attraction those trams would have been today!

And these 1935 youngsters would have loved a trip on a tram. They are Mabel Tully (now Mrs Hall) on left with Ernie Pringle and Mabel's cousins, Sheila and Jack Tully.

And these were the kind of holidaymakers and daytrippers that Newbiggin trains were bringing to the village in the late 19th century. There were ladies in their finery and children in their Sunday-best, all looking for a good time, either on the spacious beach or afloat in a pleasure craft.

It was the turn of the SS *Atiki* to run foul of the rocks off Church Point on 27th April 1903 when the Greek-owned ship ran aground in rough seas and poor visibility. Twenty-five men were taken off safely by Newbiggin Lifeboat. The captain and one other crew member remained on board and the next day were able to walk to shore at low water.

The *Anglia* Disaster

In the early hours of 9th December 1904, the Lifeboat, *Robert and Susan*, took part in what turned out to be the third major disaster to befall Newbiggin's fisherfolk. The *Anglia*, of Grinstead, Norway, was stranded on Spital Rocks with 17 crew on board. Whilst trying to give assistance, the Newbiggin coble *Henry and Jane* with eight fishermen, capsized in a heavy swell when alongside the ship. Seven of the fishermen drowned, the lone survivor being Jack Armstrong who was found clinging to a 'Dann' (a marker bouy).

By late morning, all attempts to find other survivors had failed so the Lifeboat returned to the Station. The crew of the steamer refused to leave their ship which was subsequently wrecked. The physical remnants of that disaster were to remain on the Newbiggin shoreline until June 1965 when salvage work began to remove the ship's 22-ton boilers. They had been lying as a grim reminder of the hazardous rescue attempt undertaken by the brave Newbiggin men who lost their lives.

A handful of cobles still ply their precarious trade.

The scene on that heartbreaking morning seared itself into the memory of those who were spectators. The shouting of the doomed men struggling for life in the darkness could be heard by those on shore, including their relatives who were the most anxious of the watchers. Many thousands visited Newbiggin to witness the funeral of the victims who had laid down their lives in an attempt to assist others. Artist's impression on right.

This is a sketch of Newbiggin Church and the funeral of the victims of the fishing coble disaster in December, 1904.

In one of the most memorable rescues undertaken at Newbiggin, on 22nd February 1914, Coxswain Watson Brown, aged 72, led his gallant Lifeboat crew in a rescue attempt on the stricken three-masted, full-rigged sailing ship, *Arctic Stream* (as seen in photo). In all, nineteen crew and passengers were brought to safety. Lifeboat crew members were: Coxswain Watson Brown; 2nd Coxswain Bill 'Whaler' Robinson; Bowsman John Brown; W. 'Pete' Armstrong; W. 'Calacky' Taylor; G. Jefferson; Hunter Brown; R. 'Esther Sally' Armstrong; Jack Renner; C. 'Kit' Armstrong; G. 'Common' Taylor; G. 'Dinah' Robinson; W. 'Clarkie' Taylor; W. 'Kirkhope' Robinson; J. 'Betty' Robinson; R. 'Whaler' Robinson; William Redford 'Tuff' Dawson; J. 'Jackie Grant' Armstrong and R. 'Smalt' Taylor.

This was the view that Newbiggin children had of the road leading to Dixon's Corner in 1910. The following article was compiled by Year Four of Windsor First School in 1991 and printed in the *News Post Leader* in December 1991.

'The photograph is of Newbiggin in 1910. There were no cars so they had horses and carts. The roads were only dirt tracks with no white lines. The shop on the left-hand corner is now Jasmin's. The metal railings at the bottom of the gardens were taken down in order to make weapons during the Second World War. On the right, some children are playing. They played marbles in the gutters. There is a big space where our school should be at the top of North Seaton Road. This part of Newbiggin is called 'Dixon's Corner'. It gets its name from a Mr Dixon who was the postmaster in Sidney Crescent. Some of our children walk up that road on the way to school.

'At first it was a Secondary Modern School, built in 1928 for children aged 11-14. It became a Junior School in 1963, and they placed a sundial in the quadrangle. Also the walls were blocked in around it. Our headteacher, Mrs Hunter, is retiring at Christmas. She has been here for ten years. She was head of Cleveland School, too. When she was little she lived at number 14 North Seaton Road. You can see her house on the left of the photo above. She used to go to school with Lee and Chris Hancock's grandma.'

This is how the busy road looks today with school in background.

And this is what some early 20th century children got up to – dressing up as lifeboatmen (and women). Unfortunately, we have no names for these (mostly) girls. A girl's life then, especially on becoming a fisherman's wife at Newbiggin, was extremely harsh. Living conditions in some of the fisherfolks' ramshackle houses that ran along the shore, in front of what is now Vernon Place, were deplorable. But the lady of the house struggled against the elements, and closed her eyes to the ever-present danger that ebbed and flowed only a few yards from her home.

All work and little play.

As the caption says – for children and adults alike, life in Newbiggin was 'All work and little play'.

A Special Thanks was given to the women of Newbiggin on 27th May 1927 at the Lifeboat Institution's AGM in London. One day in January that year, nearly all the members of the regular crew were out with the fishing boats, but, while they were out, a fierce gale had sprung up. The Coxswain got together a scratch crew consisting chiefly of miners who had just come off their shift at Newbiggin Colliery. With the help of twenty-five fisherwomen, wives and daughters of the men who were at sea, the Lifeboat was launched. But for the help of the women it would have been impossible to get her afloat. The boat was thrown back on to the beach and, to straighten her up, many women waded into the sea, waist deep. It was noted that this was the third time in three years in which representatives of Northumbrian fisherwomen had gone to London to be thanked for their gallantry. Photo shows Mrs Hannah Clark (on right) and Mrs Wilhelmina Dent (left) who were chosen to receive the vellum at London on behalf of the twenty-five women; both seen here with Coxswain William Robinson.

An *Evening Chronicle* reporter interviewed one of the brave women from that 1927 rescue. This is what Bella Arkle had to say: 'It was always the tradition for women to launch the Lifeboat – you had to go into the water up to your neck to get the boat out ... I was working as a cleaner when the alarm went off ... I ran to the Lifeboat house where all the women were gathering ... the weather had turned really bad when the Lifeboat was brought out ... I was up to my neck that day, but we managed to get the boat away and all the fishing boats were brought back safely.'

FLOTSAM ...

In 1868, an important development took place in the connecting of a cable between the North of England and the Continent, the landing place being near the church. In this year the first telegraphic message was transmitted through the cable to Queen Victoria. In 1880, another cable was laid through Newbiggin Cable House by the Great Northern Telegraph Company, the charge for the cables being £6 10s for 'wayleave'.

It was in 1884 that Scotsman, Mr Laing of Leith, wrote to Newbiggin Freeholders suggesting that the Moor should be utilised for the game of golf. The canny Scot enclosed a book of rules of the game and asked permission to make the necessary holes. On behalf of the Freeholders, a letter of reply was sent by Thomas Wilkie, secretary. From then on the game has prospered, the earliest games being played about 1888. A second club, Eastcliffe, the Newbiggin Workmen's Golf Club, commenced in 1885 following a meeting at the Cresswell Arms Inn, attended by several interested parties, including Dr Proudfoot of Newbiggin. As seen on photo, horses still provide natural hazards on the course.

Fishing was said to be the only 'trade' carried on in Newbiggin in 1885. Then, haddock, cod, ling, whiting, with crabs and lobsters, were said to be plentiful, as well as a few salmon trout favouring the village, whilst herring were taken in season. This late 19th century photo shows the many and varied craft that went out to ply their trade. Bulmer's brief *History of Northumberland* was published in 1887 and stated that Newbiggin township contained about 400 acres, the property of Sir A.E. Middleton of Belsay Hall; John E. Allison; J.D. Hedley and several small Freeholders. Nearby North Seaton then comprised 1,698 acres, and was the property of the representatives of the late Robert Watson Esq.

In the 1890s, one drawback for new trade entering Newbiggin was the lack of suitable accommodation for workers. Up till almost the end of the 19th century, apart from the fishing industry, there was no one to provide work for incomers nearer than North Seaton Colliery. This changed when Woodhorn Colliery was sunk in 1894 and miners from both these collieries began to look to Newbiggin for a home. Photo is looking over the rusting heapstead of No 2 Winding Gear, Woodhorn Colliery, in 1996, towards Newbiggin, where the Middle School is the white building in the distance. Over £10 million in Lottery money awarded in 2002 should soon see this building renovated.

However, when the pitmen were offered colliery houses at either North Seaton, Seaton Hirst or Ashington, then Newbiggin was the loser. Building operations were limited at Newbiggin, so expansion was seriously curtailed. Another loser was the local Co-op as their members left to join other Societies. The pitmen from the Hall family, including Sir John, lived in North Seaton, seen in our aerial photo from the 1950s.

The 1902, Kelly's Directory states that 'Newbiggin by the Sea is a watering place, a fishing village, township and chapelry in the parish of Woodhorn ... and is the terminus of a branch line from Bedlington on the Newcastle and Morpeth section of the North East Railway ... this place is now governed by an Urban District Council of seven members ... it is lighted with gas by a limited company formed in 1870 ... the chief hotel is the Old Ship and there are also several comfortable inns and lodging houses on the Cliff, affording delightful views of the sea ... fishing for salmon, haddocks, skate, codfish, codlings, soles, and flatfish is carried on; and, in the season, herrings and mackerel are taken in abundance ... the area is 339 acres of land and 297 acres of foreshore ... population in 1891 was 1,579 and in 1901 it was 2,022.' The 'lodging houses on the Cliff' might have included The Haven (above) standing majestically, 'affording delightful views of the sea ... '

The Old Ship Inn had probably one of the best views of Newbiggin Bay, looking out as it did on to the many pleasure boats lying lazily on the beach waiting for the next high tide and the next trainload of holidaymakers from Ashington and all points west.

Woodhorn Mill and Church

Written in 1891 in *North Country Lore and Legend* by J.R. Boyle

'Woodhorn is one of the bleak seaboard parishes in Northumberland. The name means 'the wooded horn' or ness of land jutting out into the sea, whereof the promontory, on which the ancient church of Newbiggin is built, forms the apex. The primeval forest has vanished and is now only represented by a few meagre-looking elms and other trees. The village of Woodhorn has been outgrown by its dependent chapelry of Newbiggin. It is a place of somewhat uninviting aspect, and its generally bare and dreary appearance is not relieved by the gaunt sail-less windmill which forms the most prominent object in the landscape.

'On coming towards the church from the village, our attention is drawn to the stone churchyard stile. I am most sorry to say that they have almost universally disappeared. Long may the church-stile be preserved. May it be jealously watched by present and future parishioners. Though we should probably find the wooden gate close beside unfastened, yet, for the respect we bear to the days of long ago, we prefer to enter the churchyard mounting the stile. Over these steps our grandmothers and grandfathers went to church. Those were picturesque times, and the lives, nay the costumes of the people were picturesque also. We may rejoice, as we ought, in the advantages of our own day, but it is worse than folly to forget to respect, and even revere, times and people that have passed away. The past of English life and history is full of poetry and romance to every true English man and woman; but I dare say the time that to most of us seems richest is the time of which the living memory of the aged has spoken in our young days.'

WOODHORN CHURCH.

On 14th October 1920, a vessel went on the rocks at the Church Point about one mile from Newbiggin. Fifteen Lifeboat crew of the *Ada Lewis*, with the help of thirty-six miners and women who hauled her into the sea, went to its assistance. On reaching the vessel after about half an hour it was discovered that it was the *Cretewheel*, a concrete tug out of the Tyne bound for Amble. The men of the Lifeboat spent a whole day standing by, then removing the unfortunate crew. But the stricken vessel was a complete wreck and, as can be seen from our recent photo, the remains of this ship, which was on its maiden voyage, are clearly visible at low tide.

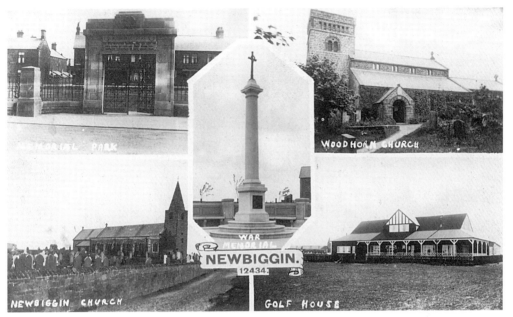

In a 1924 Guide Book on Newbiggin it was stated:

'The visitor here will find more than the ordinary charms. A long straggling street with the necessary business of a holiday resort, breaks on the right into a square which fronts a fine and capacious bay formed by two promontories of freestone. A fine stretch of sand gives ample room for parties while the fishermen welcome the demand for a boat. The fishing fleet provides more than the necessities of the home market and the auctions contribute an added attraction to the visitor. Northwards, stands the old church dedicated to St Batholomew, on a point of land that projects a considerable distance into the sea. Further north is a fine moor about two miles in extent. Here the lover of golf has a course to his heart's desire, a fine turf to tread, and the clear bracing air sweeping in from the North Sea gives a tonic and a feeling of new life to the toiler of the city.'

And there was always the lure of the brightly-painted pleasure boats.

Dolly Wray was a well-known figure in Newbiggin. She was born in 1903 and her father Jimmy Swan was on the police force in Newcastle, but prior to that he had been a fireman. Let Dolly (then aged 95) tell her own story:

'Our family was George, Mary, Tom, me and Sadie. George Swan Jnr was killed in the First World War when he was twenty-eight years old. We came to

Newbiggin in 1912 when I was nine. My mother's name was Sarah, and my father belonged North Seaton Colliery. My aunt, Angine Barrass, and my uncle, lived next door to Dr Charles Evers, the North Seaton doctor. When we came to Newbiggin we lived in Seaton Avenue – the house next door to the Presbyterian Church. I went to the little Infant's School (now Newbiggin Library) at the West End, beside the Co-op. The First World War arrived just as I was starting school. And this Army officer came into the school, saying: "I commandeer this building as a billet for my troops who have just arrived in Newbiggin. They are the Scottish Horse." They were all calvalry, you see, and they stood the whole of that first day in a long, long line, stretching right back to Spital Farm, waiting to get accommodation in the village.

Mr Peace had the Spital Farm for many years.

'So we children trooped out of school, and the teachers couldn't tell us when to come back. But that suited us fine. My friends were Annie Clark, Nellie and Lily Thistle, and Rosy Clark. We spent nearly every day on the beach, cos there was no fortifications there then. We spent our lives there with spades and pails. Norwegians used to come over every year to see to the communication cable that ran under the sea. There were three cottages on the quay wall and the Gibsons lived in one. One of the family was Matty Gibson who produced plays in Newbiggin. I believe Mrs Gibson was responsible for the cable house – she cooked for the men and saw to their quarters.

'The old family of Wray had a high-class grocery shop and the young man – as he was then – had to go in a trap to Cresswell with all the groceries for Cresswell Hall (*right*). But when they gave up that shop, Mrs Clavering took over – they had the Railway Inn as well. They had a daughter and son who spent years lying in a long chair – a beautiful lad, but sad.

'The Bertorellis came to Newbiggin just after us. They were very poor to begin with and had the little shop. A daughter, Giaconda, was a piano player and later a teacher of music. 'Mando was the son. Eventually, they made a go of it through working very hard, sometimes standing all morning, churning the ice-cream so that it would be ready for the next day. Every time there was a Pierrot Show on the beach, we were there as children, sitting in the front row. They were a hard-up affair, and Mrs Crosby took them in hand. The Crosbys had a shop at the West End.'

On the prom in the late 1930s you could have danced to the hit tunes of the day, as seen on this Bank Holiday photo below featuring the Newbiggin Accordion Band.

Mr Will Frohman's Royal Pierrots Newbiggin 1907

The Barron family arrived in Newbiggin in November 1918. John Garnett Barron had been a colliery clerk dealing with wages and compensation at Copely Colliery, Durham. He was an accomplished musician and always encouraged his son Normanton to play the organ. Once settled at Newbiggin, the father and son proceeded to put the little fishing village on the musical map by forming the Newbiggin Co-operative Orchestral Society and the Newbiggin Symphony Orchestra. Normanton Barron is seen at the organ in Ashington's Central Hall in 1932. It had originally belonged to the Miners Theatre.

Normanton obtained employment with George Arrowsmith – another Newbiggin man – who opened the department store in 1905 opposite the Grand Hotel as well as a men's outfitters next to Woolworths. On the death of George Arrowsmith in 1931, Normanton was made secretary and general manager of the newly-formed G. Arrowsmith Ltd.

On 4th May 1932, in appreciation of his services, Normanton received a gold watch which bore the inscription: 'Presented to Mr J. Normanton Barron by the choir, congregation and opera section of the Newbiggin Wesleyan Chapel in appreciation of his services 1918-31'. Normanton is seen here conducting the Newbiggin Orchestra in the bandstand on Newbiggin Promenade.

Another of Newbiggin's adopted sons was to make his mark in the world of music. John Robert (Jack) Carr (*right*) was born in 1904 in West Cornforth, County Durham. It is said that at the precise moment baby Jack was born, the local Salvation Army Band was playing at the end of the street. It was likely, therefore, that the first sound he heard was a brass band. Although not from a musical family, young Jack was soon playing the piano as well as learning a brass instrument. He took piano lessons and was soon playing the piano to accompany the silent films. The piano and the trombone – which he considered the 'King' of the brass section – became his two main instruments. But

by the age of thirty, Jack Carr wanted to conduct, and the trombone gave way to the baton when he was appointed conductor of Newbiggin Brass Band seen below in the 1920s. He arrived in Newbiggin in 1935 with wife Dora and four young children: John, Beryl, Iris and Noreen – Denis Carr was born later in Newbiggin.

They set up home initially at Moorcroft, later moving to Woodhorn Crescent when Jack got his colliery house. Photo shows Woodhorn Lane leading to Newbiggin Colliery. It was at this juncture that Jack began to study harmony, counterpoint

WOODHORN LANE, NEWBIGGIN

and composition, often into the small hours after he had finished his shift at Newbiggin Colliery. He also developed his skills as a composer and arranger, both of which he did for the Colliery Band and also for the Jack Carr Quintet which included Newbiggin men, Tommy Nichol, Dick Shepherd and Wilf Priestley. It was during World War Two that Jack suffered a serious accident at the pit. He was helping the banksman at the top of the shaft when he failed to release a lever when the cage was 'rapped away' and plunged eighty feet down the shaft. Jack suffered multiple injuries, resulting in a permanently damaged left leg.

Despite all this he played piano at local dances for the troops, and continued conducting the Newbiggin Band which by then was seriously depleted because so many members had joined the armed forces. Daughter Noreen remembers 'wonderful Sunday evenings at the house in Moorcroft when the bandsmen and their wives came and Dad played the piano for a sing-song – it was great.' When Peace was declared and brass bands began to get re-organised, Jack Carr was much in demand as a conductor and gained many successes with Bedlington Dr Pit, the Hartley Colliery Band and Wallsend Shipyard Band, conducting the latter on the radio programme *Workers' Playtime*.

Still in short pants, Denis Carr was only four when he picked up his

Denis Carr who in later life became a teacher then senior lecturer at the City of Leeds College, before joining the BBC as a radio producer. He produced *Listen to the Band* and *Bandstand* for Radio 2 and 3. He then became BBC Education Officer for the north of England. Denis is now retired and living in Derbyshire.

brother John's cornet and attempted to play a tune. Only one year later, Jack Carr began to give his youngest son tuition in reading and playing music. Such was his rapid success, Denis found himself in October 1949 playing at the Royal Albert Hall at the age of twelve. By then, young Denis was a cornetist with the Wallsend Shipyard Band and was the youngest competitor in the

National Brass Band Championship Festival. In the audience at the Albert Hall that night was none other than Princess Elizabeth, our present queen.

By this time, Jack's compostions and arrangements were being played all over the world, such as his suite, 'Four Little Maids', dedicated to four of his grandchildren. Of the many marches he wrote, 'Glemdene' was voted among the top ten contest marches of all time.

Jack also wrote a fine cornet solo called 'Gentleman Jim', dedicated to the Newbiggin-born cornet champion, Jimmy Shepherd, seen here in 1964 when he had just won the Brass Band Solo Cornet Championship for a record-breaking three times in a row.

Visitors to Newbiggin today could be entertained by the town's award-winning Greggs brass band which follows the tradition of Newbiggin Colliery Band. Popular musician, Denis Todd, blows his cornet at a recent Lifeboat Day, seated front left.

Newbiggin Tradesmen after World War Two formed a football team that played in the Mid-Week League. The photo shows that they won the cup this year *circa* 1949. Back row includes: George Davidson, J. Bell, George Eastlake, Hughie Swinburne, Harry Ricalton (brother of Frankie who ran the Railway Inn 'Rickys'), D. Sanderson, A. Cairns, Billy Sill and J. Simm. Middle row: ?, Sid McAllister, Jimmy Dodds, Joe McKenzie, George Armstrong and J. Clark. Kneeling: Billy Carr, Jay Lupton and D. Constantine.

Snaps was the rather plain name for a Newbiggin whippet that was far from being ordinary. Said Bob Moscrop, the lad in centre of photo: 'I took it to the Central Club to measure it up (it was four yards start to the inch) and then she won three handicaps out of four, running on Newbiggin Moor. *Snaps* was mated with a greyhound, and out of the litter, two won on 'flapping' tracks and another won a whippet sweep. It was Luke 'Snappy' Elswick (on left) who came from Sherburn Hill to live in Newbiggin's Marine Street. He brought the bitch with him. The man on the right is Georg'a Smith from Moor Estate – he was a coal filler at Newbiggin Colliery.'

The Wallaw Cinema at Newbiggin was always called 'Carters' because of its connection with Newbiggin man, Carlton Carter. His daughter, Betty, an avid film buff, used her free pass practically every night of the week. She remembers that, in the early days of cinema, children could gain admission by handing in two jam jars. At some matinees, each paying child was given a counter which gave them free admission for their next visit. Film breaks and projectionist's errors simply added to the fun of a visit to the magical moving pictures. One night, Betty says that the villain in *Lorna Doone* was slain in one reel, only to turn up riding a horse, quite unharmed, in the next. Photo shows scaffolding being put in place prior to knocking the old cinema down.

Cinema-going peaked in the immediate post-Second World War years and Betty helped her father Carlton to pack over seven hundred people into the Newbiggin Wallaw – 'to get them in out of the cold.' By then, Walter Lawson owned not only five Ashington cinemas, but those at Newbiggin, Bedlington, Morpeth, Blyth and Alnwick; he also booked films for Berwick and Gallashiels. After closing as a cinema in the early 1960s, and ending its Bingo connection in the 1970s, the Wallaw Cinema acted as a store-room for a few years before being finally demolished in 1994 and a block of flats built on the site.

'THE NEW ERA'

RAILWAY STATION - NEWBIGGIN.

There were many seaside resorts that benefited with the coming of the railways, and Newbiggin was no exception. At weekends the trains were packed with visitors old and young, spilling their human cargoes out like grains of silver sand upon the platform at Newbiggin Railway Station. What matter if the mucky coal screening plant was only yards away. It was the start of an adventure that would provide a lifetime of memories.

This is how the *Morpeth Herald* reported the day the new promenade opened:

'Today will be a red letter day in the rich and varied history of Newbiggin when the village officially embarks upon a new era, which, given the average amount of luck, and wise administration by the local authority, will be one of steady progress and constant development.

'On the 28th day of May 1932, the promenade was officially opened by Sir Charles Trevelyan, Lord Lieutenant of the County. Thus will some historian of the future write, and he will be right in selecting this important event for special mention. Indeed, it will provide an admirable opening for a new chapter of the History of Newbiggin, with the title *The New Era.*'

There were two ceremonies that day. One at the Quay Wall by Sir Charles, and the other at the new Bathing Shelter, opened by Cllr Willie McLean who said: 'No longer will there be a necessity for mothers of children and the old people to rush from the sands and take the train home at the first sign of rain. This shelter ('bottom' shelter seen on left of photo) with accommodation for several hundred people will do away with all this.'

But if you were one of the 6,904 folks living in Newbiggin in 1935 who wanted to go to Newcastle, either by bus or train, you would probably have travelled in a carriage behind an old-fashioned long-funnelled engine like this above. Here are some of the times and prices that would concern you. Research done by Colin Wanless from Reid's *Railway Guide*, 1935. The bus route by United Automobile Services from Newcastle Haymarket was via Seaton Burn, Bedlington, Choppington, Guide Post, Stakeford, North Seaton, Ashington and Newbiggin.

The station was always busy right up till it closed in the 1960s.

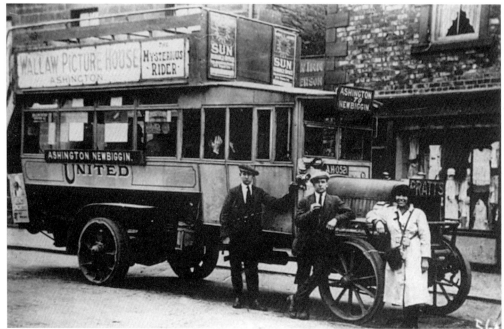

This was the first ever bus to travel between Newbiggin and Ashington in the early 1920s. The driver and conductress were David and Lillian Henderson who later married the local policeman, Sgt McCormick. Man on left is Freddy Hays, United Bus Company's first inspector. The bus was, in effect, a World War One lorry with windows inserted and an 'upstairs' built on. The journey by bus to Newcastle in 1935 took 65 minutes and cost 1s 5d Single, and 2s 1d Return. First bus from Newbiggin to the Haymarket left through the week at 6.05 am and on Sundays at 10.20 am. Bus services to Newbiggin after 12 noon were usually every 15 minutes. The last bus from the Haymarket on a Saturday (which is what interested a lot of Newbiggin folk who attended the Oxford Galleries) was at 11.30 pm.

Average train journeys in 1935 from Manors to Newbiggin took just under an hour and cost 2s 2d for a First Class Single; and a Third Class Single was 1s 5d; Return 2s 0d. The train stopped at Jesmond, West Jesmond, South Gosforth, Benton, (almost the same as today's Metro), Backworth, Seghill, Seaton Delaval, Hartley, Newsham, Bebside, Bedlington, North Seaton and Ashington. After 8.00 am there was one train an hour leaving Manors for Newbiggin at 24 mins past the hour. From Newbiggin, there was also one train an hour, leaving at 40 mins past the hour. (Cartoon by Ron Herdman of the *Ashington Advertiser*.)

Going out of Newbiggin, this was the view you would have of the platform. On far right, a coal truck is being loaded from a railway wagon, near the weighbridge.

First train out of Manors for Newbiggin was at 5.37 am, arriving 7.05 am.
Last train out of Manors for Newbiggin was at 10.54 pm, arriving at 11.51 pm.
First train the other way left at 6.43 am, arriving at Manors at 7.37 am.
Last train the other way left Newbiggin 9.40 pm, arriving at Manors at 10.40 pm.

And the last train from Newbiggin in the mid-1960s would have looked something like this ... a diesel. Note the Newbiggin Colliery screens towering high in the background (demolished 1965) and Long Park houses so close on right.

A young Ned Mather with his friends Ernie Anderson, Willie Ross, Arthur Lewis and Charlie Watson at Newbiggin County Modern School around 1933 doing a spot of gymnastics on the lawn. The New or 'Top' Ship was then a Younger's house. On the left, over the road, is the building that was then occupied by Thompson's Stores, now the Apostolic Church.

Newbiggin man, seventy-seven-year-old Eddie Groves, recalls as a young lad when all the Colliery School children were let out of class for a special occasion. Eddie says: 'We all walked down to the wooden fence, and soon this great big ship passed by the huts that were built below the school. It was the *Mauretania* seen above on its way from the Tyne to be scrapped.'

The date was 1st July 1935 and one of the fastest and most elegant ships afloat was on its way to Rosyth in Scotland where all the fittings were to be auctioned off.

"The Bungalows", Newbiggin-by-Sea.

And these were the 'Huts' that Eddie mentioned. In fact their correct title was East Lea Bungalows. Note that first one has life-saving equipment hanging on wall.

John White remembers: 'The Rocket Gun, based near the Lifeboat House, was fired to summon the crew and those prepared to help with the launch of the lifeboat. Although there were cases when large ships were in distress, in the majority of cases the concern was for Newbiggin's own cobles. Groups of people would gather at the Lifeboat House, or on the Church Point. On a personal note, I remember family distress at the fate of the Dawson's coble, *Universal*, which was lost on 28th September 1940. One of the widows, Georgina, was my godmother, and my grandmother was a Dawson.' (In photo John is seen on left with brother Len, Betty and Les outside their home at Homelyn House.)

World War Two hit home with a vengeance on Friday 7th November 1941. The following is taken from an ARP report in the Northumberland Aviation Diary:

'One aircraft flew in from the sea, very low, with its navigation lights on. It dropped two 250-kg High Explosives at Newbiggin-by-the-Sea, killing three civilians outright and three who died later. One soldier, Pte Lamb of the Cheshire Regiment, was also killed. One bomb struck the roadway at the junction of Simonside Terrace and Front Street. It ricocheted into the front garden of number 34 Front Street and exploded. Houses were damaged at the rear of Springfield Terrace and, on Front Street, were completely demolished, others at either side were extensively damaged. In all, 180 buildings were damaged.

Photo shows Heinkel bomber entering coast over North Seaton with the Hirst Colliery rows in centre. (Note – an even earlier bomb, dropped on Sunday 16th February 1941, had exploded 20 yards out to sea, blowing in the windows of houses near the Church Point.)

Laurie Dent (now living in Wideopen) remembers the day that Newbiggin came under attack from the German bomber:

'There were seven people killed by the bomb that dropped in November 1941. My father, who worked at the colliery under Mr Arthur Peebles, was a civil defence instructor, qualifying in 1937. The old Salvation Army Hall was turned into a temporary mortuary, and father had the job of putting the bodies in order. The bomber flew so low that the bomb hadn't time to attain the vertical trajectory. The indentation of where it bounced was visible for many years on the slope leading to Simonside Terrace.'

Tommy Nichol was living at No 8 Allison's Yard when the bomb dropped. He was blown half way across the room. Tommy played for Woodhorn Colliery Band and also North Seaton. He also played in Jack Carr's Novelty Brass Quintet on BBC Radio. Billy Cotton tried to lure him done to London when Tommy moved out of Newbiggin in 1963. But he declined – he was getting more money at the pit at Cotgrave, Notts. Tommy's son Malcolm, still living in Cotgrave, recalls that he played as a young lad on the tanks that stood on Newbiggin Moor during World War Two. They were used as target practice for our own Spitfires and Hurricanes.

Entrance and Drive, Newbiggin. North Seaton and District Social Club Bank House.

Dorothy Harold (née Brown), now living in Nottingham, recalls:

'We were living at the Bank House Lodge on the evening the bomb dropped. My father Marshall Brown was the gardener for the Newbiggin, North Seaton and District Social Club, as it was called then. Dad was putting coal on the greenhouse fire, but he managed to get out and ran on to the road where he helped to look after two ladies who had just come out of Dr Angus' surgery. They were in a terrible state – we later found an axe-head in our garden, so Dad had a lucky escape, thanks to the high wall.' (On our photo, a majestic entrance to the Bank House is seen with Lodge on left – now a council office.)

'After the war we moved out of the Lodge into Welfare Crescent, next door to my friend Irene Algar. In this photo of my dad with Irene, she had just received a new bike, so me, my dad and Irene went cycling up the coast – I took the photo.'

Dorothy also sent the rent agreement between her father and Hilton Dawson, secretary of the Bank House then. It is dated 11th November 1938 and is for an annual rent of £26 paid in ten shillings per week instalments. Part of Marshall Brown's duties were: 'To keep the grass cut short and borders trimmed between the boundary wall of Jubilee Terrace on the south, and the Lodge wall on the north, and from the entrance gates to the west, to the front of the Bank House, and the remainder boundaries to the Prom to be cut at least twice per annum.'

The agreement signed by Landlord H. Dawson also stated: 'All flower beds to be planted with flowering plants in season, and such flowers to be the property of the Club. The remainder of the land belonging to the Club under cultivation, with the exception of that portion let to the Steward, may be cultivated to the tenant's own advantage.'

Local character Johnnie Storey stands with his horse and cart beside the Lodge at Bank House.

Dorothy continued:

'The Lodge wasn't all that big with a small bedroom at the back and a larger one that held two beds at the front. There was a kitchen but no sitting room – just a scullery. As well as gardening, Dad had to go to work at the Pit. He kept livestock in the garden such as chickens and rabbits which he bred for meat in the winter – we also had a pony which was used to fetch sea coal. I loved it there.'

This was the Bank House Committee sitting outside the club with the sea behind them in the 1950s. Back left: ?, ?, Billy Gay, Ernie Price, Tommy Bowness, ?. Front: ?, Percy Bennett, Hilton Dawson, Ted Mather and ? McCall.

Some more recent committee men. From left Walter Turnbull, Jackie Jennings, Ken Armstrong; Jimmy Costello and Jackie Johnson.

If you go back a century and a half, you can find reports of over 30 cobles fishing out of Newbiggin. Nowadays you can almost count them on one hand. The local fishing industry is not helped by government legislation that continues to curtail the salmon season and makes it impossible for a salmon licence to be passed on from father to son. But for the moment that does not worry the *Endeavour's* owner and skipper, Jimmie Dawson, holding aloft a magnificent salmon caught by drift netting. On the left is his crewman, Mark Stephenson. Photo by John Tickner who specialises in travel, industrial and commercial photography. He is a recent winner of a Ballantines International Photography Award. On the front cover of this book is another of John's photos featuring sea-coaler Joe Smith and his horse and cart working off 'The Spirals' at Newbiggin.

SECTION FOUR

SANDSHOE DAYS

Ask any child of the 1940s and '50s what their favourite footwear was and they would shout: 'Sandshoes!' Costing one shilling and elevenpence ha'penny from the market, they were probably their mam's favourite, too. And asked where they would like to spend a sunny Sunday afternoon, the unanimous decision of children from the outlying district would be 'Newbiggin!' Above you see the girls of Newbiggin Middle School entertaining the crowd in the mid-1990s with their Irish Dancing. They were putting their best foot forward, not wearing any old sandshoes, but expensive dancing pumps that complemented their Emerald green skirts and white tops.

Rose Hails (née Stokoe) recalls her 1946 backstreet trip to Newbiggin:

'Eleanor Douglas was my best friend and lived next door to us in Welfare Crescent, Ashington. Selby Douglas, her dad, was part owner of a horse and cart – the horse's name was Neddy, and it was stabled down at the allotment along with the cart. It was used to transport anything from furniture to horse manure.

'The summer of '46 was to be the first of many seaside outings to Newbiggin via this vehicle. The beaches had only recently been cleared of barbed wire and ammunition left from the throes of war. The nearest beach to us was at the Chain, later named Sandy Bay. Those days always seemed to dawn bright and sunny. An excited group of children cheered loudly as Selby drove Neddy into the street. The cart was all cleaned up and a tarpaulin covered the floor - this became our shelter if it rained. Our mothers helped us aboard then handed up our baits and bottles of water. Money – if any – was clubbed together for a bottle of Tizer and a pennorth of Oxos bought at Betty's corner-end shop. Sandwiches varied from jam, sauce, chutney, treacle and sugar. For the lucky ones there was cheese, egg, Spam or dripping.

'By now, my oldest sister Joan, would be looking wistfully at us. But being rather lady-like, declined to join us, saying: "I am not goin' on that smelly cart and dirty horse." Which was all quite true, but it didn't bother us. Then we were off as Selby shouted: "Gee up, Neddy!" And our mothers waved with sighs of relief at having us out of the way for a whole day. Selby led us children in a sing-song, from *Roll out the Barrel* to *Onward Christian Soldiers*, only stopping to shout: "Hang on there, wa gannin ower a bump." As the cart had no sides, we held hands to avoid falling off, amid shrieks of laughter. We rarely saw a bus or car, so there was no danger from traffic.'

NEWBIGGIN BY THE SEA, FRONT STREET.

Our 1930s photo shows a policeman overseeing a traffic-free Newbiggin Front Street.

Needle's Eye Rocks, Newbiggin. 11352.

'After collecting firewood for Selby's campfire, we went off to explore, to jump the sand-dunes, play leapfrog, and popular ball games before collecting willicks on the rocks. Selby blew a whistle to tell us that bait was ready. Then we congregated around the fire where the brew of tea was always strong, flavoured with condensed milk, and made in a large billycan. The willicks were placed in a pail of salted water to be boiled for tea-time. The tiny shellfish were picked from the shell with a safety pin, and the afternoon flew as we repeated the morning's escapades. (On our photo you could search for willicks on the rocks beside the Needle's Eye).

'It seemed unbelievable that a large group of children could be chaperoned by one dad, and no harm befell us. We always came home tired but happy. Sadly, children of today have no such freedom. Selby Douglas and our parents are long gone, and now I am of the older generation with grandchildren of my own who like to hear me when I become nostalgic for all those Sandshoe Days.'

Dolly Wray also remembers those days:

'During the Second World War there were lots of troops billeted in Newbiggin. Among the first to come was the Cheshire Regiment, then the Shropshire. Miss Clark had the house called Moor End House. The military took that over as well. In Homelyn House, where the Crawfords lived, they took that over. The Haven on the sea front where Sir Charles Trevelyan had lived – the troops took that over. The Army were not there all that long, they just did their training and off they went. Newbiggin used to be a lovely place with a beautiful beach and all the fishing boats. But during the Second World War all the fortifications were put up on the beach. After that, the subsidence from the colliery fettled things. The colliery surveyor, Mr Jed Brown, told me that they were working a mile out to sea. Before Jed it was Percy Brown, and my father always went with him.'

The Beach, Newbiggin 12203

Margaret Norman recalls her early days in Newbiggin, after arriving as a young post-war bride from the Leicestershire rural village of Countesthorpe:

'The contrast between my home village, surrounded as it was by trees of oak and copper beech, and the gardens ablaze with colour, could not have been greater, and I hated it. Newbiggin had no trees. A long straight street down which the cold wind whirled, its bitterness nearly cutting you in two. At one end was the railway station hidden behind ugly billboarding, and opposite, a small park of grimy grass, the inscription above the gates proclaiming it a 'Memorial to Our Glorious Dead.' Tall grey stone Victorian houses lined the street. Nothing bright, just never ending greyness. The small front gardens, with struggling plants and tiny lawns of sooty grass. The whole overshadowed by the pit heap and screens and the winding gear of the colliery and, over all, a pall of grey smoke belching from every chimney.'

Front St. Newbiggin.

Photo shows the entrance to the Railway Station. Just leaving are two small girls in boaters that might have been part of their uniform while attending Mr Sandiford's Private School whose advert in the *Morpeth Herald* in 1900 stated: 'Train service is convenient for day pupils'.

Margaret continues: 'Further on, the shops, most looking run down and uninviting and requiring a lick of paint – and the pubs – so many for one small village. The Top Ship – Railway – Ship Hotel – Coble – Queen Victoria – Cresswell Arms – Dolphin. Mining is thirsty work. At the corner of the shops on the cobbled stones stood a disused pump, a reminder that tap water had been a luxury at this end of the village until a few years ago. Past the Co-op and the cinema, you came to small streets of tired-looking terraced houses behind which rag clippie rugs were beaten free of dust, and the washing strung across the lanes, until the arrival of a tradesman's cart or the coals made the pinny-clad housewives dash out to take in their spotless sheets before they could be covered in black dust.

'At this end of the village were also the fisherfolk's cottages, clustering round the Lifeboat house. A close-knit community, dressed mainly in black. The men in dark gansies and the women in long black shirts and shawls, black stockings and shoes or, more often, carpet slippers or sandshoes.

'In front of the cottages, the sandy bay, lashed by the merciless grey North Sea. The wheels of the cobles waiting for their return from the fishing, perhaps with a child rocking on them, until the fishermen nearing the beach jumped into the sea, and helped to manoeuvre the boats on to the wheels. Then their wives, who had been waiting in little groups by the lifeboat house awaiting the men's return, waded into the sea – their long black skirts clinging to them, and two to each boat would grasp the heavy ropes attached to the wheels and haul the cobles ashore – up beyond the water line – ropes over their shoulders – backs bent as they trudged up the sands. The men waded ashore carrying the fish boxes containing their precious catch, shoulder high.

'The Church jutted out at one end of the bay, a landmark to sailors – the graveyard a resting place for many of them. "Found drowned – Dear husband of Bella." The rocks below the Church

Point were rough with mussels clinging tenaciously. These were the bait for the lines and guarded jealously by the fisherfolk. Any unsuspecting visitor to the village who decided to pick mussels would be told in no uncertain terms by an angry fisherwoman dashing across the sands to "Gan to Hell and leave wor mussels be."

'Behind the Church, north and away from the village, spread the Moor and golf links, an oasis of springy grass and bright sea pinks in a grey landscape. On the right, the sea, and the flat Fairy Rocks. On the left, overshadowing the roofs of the huddled houses – the pit heap.

The Motor Boats, Newbiggin. 10896

'When summer came, the sands were the place to be. Andy Stewart's Shuggy Boats were brought out and a little painted merry-go-round, turned by hand, with donkeys waiting for small riders. Ferry boats, not cobles, stood on their wheels alongside home-made stages. When children and mothers and dads had lined up and climbed along the stages and been steadied into a seat round the sides of the boat, the engine was started up with a quick pull on its rope and off they chugged for a breezy trip round the bay.

The Promenade, Newbiggin.

'That was when I began to enjoy myself. My husband's uncle Tom owned the boat *Try Again*, and I wheedled him to let me take the tiller. "See that chimney? Steer for it." It was great. Living here wasn't so bad after all. The sun did shine, not so warmly as at home, but I could put up with that as long as the brightness lightened the main street. Now, years later, the main street has grassy flowerbeds ablaze with colour in the summer. The houses and shops all have fresh white paint, the pit and its ugly heap have gone, also the station and its camouflage of bill hoarding. The atmosphere is not quite so murky and, after fifty years, this is where I call *Home*.'

The ancient custom of 'Riding The Boundaries' by Newbiggin Freeholders was observed in June 1949 and the ceremony of 'dunting' a Freeholder in accordance with ancient rites was performed for the benefit of a class of scholars from the Newbiggin County School. At the Dunting Stone, Mr Adam Storey, 96 years old, and Newbiggin's Grand Old Man, was again 'dunted'.

After the proclamation, a bagful of nuts was scattered on the ground and the children scambled for them. This was the first time this part of the ceremony had been observed since just prior to the second war. A short history of the Freeholders was given by Mr J.F. Gibson, secretary, and by Mr Storey himself who explained that the Charter was granted by King John in recognition of the services given to him and the Crown by the inhabitants of Newbiggin. The Freeholders in olden days carried out many of the functions now performed by the local authority. They appointed their constables, bailiffs and ale-tasters. The records of the ancient courts between 1600 and 1700 mentioned that one Newbiggin man was fined twelve shillings for 'brewing insufficient ale'.

Naa, pet, that's not the Duntin' Styen. (From 1926 *Ashington Colliery Magazine*.)

In days gone by, the custom of riding the bounds had been done on horseback, but in modern days this has given way to the motor car. Some of the Freeholders claimed the land by walking from the Dunting Stone to St Bartholomew's Church. Adam Storey, then the oldest living Freeholder, recalled the day when he used to attend the ceremony as a youngster in bare feet. Another veteran there was 85-year-old William Robinson who had also been a Freeholder for many years. It was the custom when horses were used to assemble on the Moor and take part in a series of horse races. For the schoolchildren, who were accompanied by their headmaster Mr James Wood and Mr Tait, the ceremony was full of interest and the reason for their visit was the introduction to their education of local history subjects.

The 'Modern School' (or Dixon's Academy as some pupils called it) was also the venue for Newbiggin Youth Club, which began around 1949/50. Edna Armstrong (née Hogg) remembers that as a young girl she was the first secretary, and another prominent committee member was Tom Hogg. Some of the teachers from the school, such as Tom Swailes and Mr Jackson, helped out, but the organisation was left mainly to the young members. The first teacher/warden who assisted was Sid Robson who played rugby for Ashington; and Valerie Tully, the County Youth Organiser, also played a major role supporting young people in the district.

On right *Ashington Post* photo and article on Tommy Hogg of Newbiggin. Tommy was a young farm worker in 1950. He played a leading part in the physical training and boxing groups. He was also a member of the cricket, cycling, camping, swimming and games section. Warden Sid Robson had this to say about Tommy: 'He has the welfare of the club at heart, and when he has a job to do, members can rest assured that it will be thoroughly done.'

Edna Armstrong said: 'We had the run of the whole school, but never once was there any vandalism or rowdy behaviour. We met once a week to begin with, but soon we were meeting about three times, having a barn dance, playing games or ordinary dancing. During school holidays we met on the Moor and played outdoor games such as cricket.'

Personality—5

Newbiggin Youth Club President

PRESIDENT of Newbiggin Youth Club is 21-year-old Tommy Hogg, a farm worker, and his efforts on behalf of members are well appreciated by everyone.

Tommy plays a leading part in the physical training and boxing groups, and is also a member of the cricket, cycling, camping, swimming and games sections.

Even with all these outdoor interests, he still finds time to serve on the club committee, and he took part in last year's Ashington Youth Week.

Mr S. J. Robson, Newbiggin Youth Centre's warden-teacher, has this to say of him: "Tommy has the welfare of the club at heart, and when he has a job to do members can rest assured that it will be thoroughly done"

In 1951 the Youth Club took part in a procession through Newbiggin. The boys thought they would emulate Newcastle United – who had just won the FA Cup that year – by donning black and white strips which they borrowed from Ashington FC. They are seen here on a cart being hauled along by a horse. Standing with 'cup' is Billy Armstrong. Also included are: 'Boxer' Armstrong, Colin Graham, Bob Armstrong, Jack Dodds, Tommy Regan, Bob Dickman, Bob McCall, Alan Lowery, Jim Storey and a lad named Wake. Man on pavement in trilby hat is Willie O'Neal, woman with dark hair at phone box is Bob and Bill's mum Gladys Armstrong. The procession is seen passing Newbiggin Railway Station with Buteland Terrace in background. Does anyone know the junior 'nurses' on the wagon?

And this is Newbiggin Health Centre that now stands on the site of the old railway station.

A Youth Club Christmas Party in 1951 at the County Modern School, included are: Pat Dinsdale, Florence Main, Brenda Glasper, Norman McCall, Sid Robson (teacher/warden), Colin Graham, Doris Moore, 'Tot' Aisbitt, Jean Hall, Tommy Hogg, Ronnie Eastlake, Mary Dawson, Patricia Brown, Joyce Atkinson, Rosemary Mackenzie, Basil Brown, Sally Oliver, Duncan Swinney, Jimmy Hughes, Betty Spears, Hazel Robinson, Ann Lincoln, Joan Guthrie, Doris Bulloughs, Doreen Spowart, Arnold Emery, Irene Algar, Eileen Storey, Betty Hedley, Barbara Bowden, Alan Simpson, Jim Storey, Joan Turnbull, Edna Hogg (who provided photo), Valerie Tully (County Youth Organiser), James Wood (headteacher), Mrs Wood, Peter Marshall, Alan Turnbull, Ken Covell, Bob Armstrong, Thornton Armstrong, Robin Bell and Willie Patterson.

In 1952 Newbiggin Presbyterian Church Junior Choir took part in a concert. Also appearing were Ivy Whitelaw and father William, on right. Seated centre, 15-year-old Laura Gray was producer and pianist. Other adults helping out included Mr and Mrs Dingwall, Mrs Lilburn and Mrs Walker (the choir conductors).

When the seaside town of Newbiggin takes a stranger to its heart then you can bet that he or she has done something outstanding to earn that privilege. One such a man was Australian aborigine boxer, Dave Sands, who arrived in Newbiggin, extremely homesick, in 1949. Because of a connection with local man, Ernie Bates, who was chef at the Newcastle hotel in which Sands was staying while training for a fight at St James' Hall, Dave soon became a familiar figure around the little seaside town. When he fought in Newcastle and London, his career was followed with great interest by the fisherfolk. One of six fighting brothers, Dave was a contender for the world title, held then by Jake LaMotta, and showed he had the right credentials when he knocked out Britain's Dick Turpin in one round. Sadly, Dave Sands never did get that title fight as he was killed in a driving accident back in Australia in August 1952. His son David is seen beside the memorial erected to Dave's memory in 1988.

Here is a part of a poem written by Australian Delma Rose Clark whose husband Michael is probably the leading authority on boxing 'Down Under' ...

You talk about your heroes, and how they used their hands,
The greatest of your idols was a boxer named Dave Sands.
A dusky-skinned young axeman, from Kempsey way he came,
To try his luck in the boxing ring that led him into fame.

... Dave went on to greater heights, won titles by the score,
Many champions felt his great left hook, and hit the canvas floor.
This modest, shy, quiet country boy, made his mark in history,
But I know his heart was always home, back with his family.

CO-OPERATION AND COALMINING

FRONT STREET - NEWBIGGIN.

The year of 1863 saw the inauguration of the Newbiggin Co-operative 'Store'. The pioneering work of the Co-operative Movement locally had been carried out at North Seaton Colliery Village, but because of a covenant stating that only one shop could be allowed on the whole estate, the determined men of North Seaton established their first shop in Newbiggin when some premises, leased from John Downie for seven years at an annual rental of £16, were opened on Front Street in March 1863. Eventually, the barrier at North Seaton was overcome and a branch opened there in November 1874. New premises were rebuilt in 1913. In 1908 a branch began at Cleveland Street, and in 1914 the 'Arcade' premises on Newbiggin's High Street were opened. In 1920, the Society bought the farm at 'Woodhorn Demesne' and soon commenced the delivery of milk. In later years it dispensed with its farming operations, but continued to deliver milk from their dairy with A. Elliott as depot foreman. Photo taken around 1890, shows Newbiggin Co-operative premises on right, next to a newsagents, then J. Buddles confectionery shop.

Because of the spiralling growth of colliery houses, it was decided in 1920 to build new Co-op premises at the 'colliery end' of Newbiggin. In effect, this was little more than an Army hut, but the branch was rebuilt in 1936 and modernised in 1957 when a bakery was opened adjoining the store. The butchery department at Newbiggin Co-op, under manager Percy Bennett, slaughtered and prepared live stock in its own abbatoir. Travelling shops went all around the district, doing a good trade. Catering requirments for weddings, socials and dances etc was carried out in the Co-operative Hall on Front Street. A pharmacist, Mr A.G. Wallace MPS, was appointed in January 1955 as manager of the pharmacy at 97 Front Street. The 'Old Store Yard' photo was taken recently, but directly ahead was where the 'killing shops' were situated – now used to stable horses.

Mr Bill Denton was appointed manager when the Co-op began its own Works Department in 1933. Most of the improvements to the Society's buildings were made by Bill and his team with J. Lawson as foreman. Bill Denton, as funeral director, was also responsible for the Society's funeral arrangements, carried out 'with dignity and sincerity' at all times.

The last of the Newbiggin Co-operative Stores was built on Spital Estate and opened in 1955, but a newly-erected Drapery Department opened in the early 1960s at 85 Front Street with Mr A. Dixon as manager. At that time there were also Drapery shops at North Seaton Colliery, and 202 Milburn Road, Ashington. As stated in its centenary booklet, published in 1963: 'Bespoke tailoring is a speciality'. At the offical opening of the Newbiggin Drapery were, from left, Mr Carrick, Alec Dixon, Willie Maclean, Jim York and Jim Batey.

Newbiggin Colliery

In an attempt to find coal, boring had commenced at The Carrs in Newbiggin in 1902 by Wood Brothers of Morpeth. Photo shows building work in 1908. The following details concerning the colliery were compiled by an electrician there, the late James Victor 'Vic' Hughes, married to Hannah Waite, who lived in North View, Newbiggin. In 1907, the first sod was cut by Mrs Davidson to commence sinking of two shafts.

No 1 shaft was to be sunk 95 fathoms (570 ft) to the Main Seam then down to the Yard Seam – a total depth of 106 fathoms.

On 9th August 1909, during the sinking of the shaft, one of the sinkers, Mr E. Boldon, aged thirty, fell from the kibble into the sump and was drowned. An attempted rescue by Mr Arthur Peebles, gained him a medal at a later date. On 14th October 1910, No 1 shaft commenced drawing coal, and that same month Sinkers Row was erected. William Warbeck, aged 41, was the first man to be killed underground at Newbiggin Colliery. A Screening Plant was built about one mile from the pit-head. Railway sidings were laid adjacent to the Railway Station. Tubs were hauled from the pit-head to the Screens and back by a stationary engine using the endless-rope system. Chains were wound around the rope with one link fastened to the tub by means of a steel pin.

From the moment the shaft was sunk on Newbiggin Carrs, there was an uneasy alliance between the fishermen and the miners. This was borne out in this 1926 J. Short cartoon of a man walking into the sea with his towel and bar of soap, above the caption: 'Hoo did they knaa Aa was a filler at the colliery?' Note, it was always considered unhealthy for a miner to wash his back as it 'weakened' him.

PITHEAD BATHS

"THE WETTERS NOT DORTY, TYEK YOR CAP OFF!!"

In 1910, a workingmen's club was built in Newbiggin and called 'The Central Club'. Photo shows a late 1930's Central committee plus members of the Whippet Club. Kneeling: Joe Whitehall, Marki Williams and Tom 'Bat' Bell. Also included are: Harry Graham, Bennett, Bob Williams, Andrew Dickman, George Hedley, Dick Callan, Bob Hewitson, George Taylor, Jim Filler the steward plus his wife Margaret, G.R. 'Taffy' Storey, Jim Adams, Tut Storey, Billy Nicholson and Tom Graham.

Some Colliery Officials when the pit opened included:

Agent – R.O. Brown;
Manager – R. Kellett;
Overmen – S. Hornsby, H. Clark, P. Spooner & S. Ferral;
Master Shifter – Jack Gowlands;
Engineeers – R. Bainbridge, W. Gladys & T. Manley;
Master Blacksmith – Jack Kenny;
Master Joiner – W. Coates;
Storehouse Keeper – James Oram;
Head Horsekeeper – James Punton;
In charge of sinking shafts – Dod Green & J. Rodham;
Winding Enginemen – T. Charlton, W. Endean, J. Farrow & J. Hindmarsh;
Banksmen – Arthur Peebles, W. Jamieson & P. Dawson.

In August 1924, pit-head baths were built for the miners consisting of showers. Having changed into his pit clothes, the miner put away his clean clothes, attached them to a rope, and they were pulled up into the roof space where they were kept dry by hot-water pipes. Later, an addition was built on with more showers and lockers in which the clothes were kept dry by hot air. Bath Attendants – G. Gibb, T. Batch and T. Foster.

A Canteen was then built, enabling the men to obtain hot drinks at the beginning and end of their shift. All this building work was carried out by colliery tradesmen under the supervison of the Engineer, J. Manley. Plans were drawn up by colliery surveyors under Jed Brown. Brickwork – J. Endean, T. Williams and W. Armstrong; Steelwork – H. Dawson, J. Kenny and W. Brydon; Joinery – W. Coates, J. McCallum and D. Armstrong; Plumbing – T. Beale; Electrical – J. Cook and J.V. Hughes (our writer) and Painting – Billy Wray.

A group of Canteen staff are seen in the late 1940s. Back from left: Grace Paton, Jim Manley, Dot Thornton and Doreen Storey. Front: Mary Adams, Meggy Barber and Linda Taylor.

For many years, ponies were used underground until, over a period of time, electrical mechanisation followed, and with the use of conveyor belts, coal-cutting machines and haulage engines, the ponies were withdrawn. When electrical winding engines began to be used, coal was drawn up the shaft at 33 ft per second, and for man-riding slowed down to 28 ft per second.

Up until 1862 it was usual for a coalmine to have only one shaft. But that year a pumping beam broke at the top of a shaft at the New Hartley Pit, completely blocking the shaft. No one could get down – no one could come up. There were 204 men and boys down the pit that day. By the time the rescuers reached them, ten days had elapsed and they found all of them, dead in each other's arms. It took that disaster to make it compulsory to have two shafts in every mine. Talk about closing the coal house door ...

At the turn of the 20th century, many mining
families began to move into the area. It was
coal that brought them from Cornwall,
Cumberland, Ireland and Scotland. One
incoming Scottish family were the Nesbits
who journeyed down from Motherwell to
sink their roots into the fertile Newbiggin
soil. George and Jane Nesbit had two sons,
Robert and young George, both of whom
worked at Newbiggin Colliery until they
retired at 65 years of age. Robert Nesbit
married Annie Dent, a fisher lass. George
also married a local girl, and he went on to
become a miners' union official at Newbiggin
Colliery and also became chairman of
Newbiggin UDC. George Nesbit is seen here
wearing his badge of office which shows the
original Newbiggin crest of an anchor
entwined by a rope.

Jack Adams came to Newbiggin by way of the collieries at Wallsend and
Netherton. In 1924 he became chairman of Newbiggin Miners' Lodge and was
a Labour councillor for many years. Jack took a great interest in Newbiggin
Children's Sports Committee and also served on the committee at the Central
Club. He died at the age of seventy-three. Jack Adams, seen on left, in his
capacity as Newbiggin Miners' secretary, hands over a long-service certificate
to John Spooner who had been in the mines for sixty-two years. Also featured
are left J. Wilkinson, Newbiggin Colliery under-manager, Cllr George Nesbitt,
Mr J.W.B. Gair mine manager, Alderman J. Mordue, Labour Officer to No 3
Area of the NCB, stands far right – others not named. Jim Adams, eldest son of
the above, a mines inspector representing the workmen, was elected to
Newbiggin Council in 1940, and served as a county councillor for ten years.
Living at No 4 Spital Crescent, Jim's health deteriorated after the fire at
Lynemouth Colliery in 1966 and he died soon afterwards.

By the time Newbiggin Colliery opened, pit ponies had been on the scene for many years. The strong, sturdy animals were ideal for pulling materials down the pit where it was too low for machinery to operate. The ponies were kept in underground stables in whitewashed stalls, kept meticulously clean by the horsekeepers. One such man was James Punton whose son, Ernest Punton, is seen at horse's head, hauling a tub.

When any new pit was being sunk, a row of houses, invariably named 'Sinkers' Row', was built to accommodate these daring men who put their lives at risk every time they descended the new shaft in a 'kibble'. But it was

the residents' lives that were at risk when a disastrous fire gutted the entire row of wooden shacks in 1934. Inset in our photo is one of the miners' wives.

A Mechanics Institute has existed in Newbiggin since 1891, and five years later it had 150 members. It appears that the membership must have been swelled by men who either worked at Woodhorn or North Seaton collieries. The president, according to the 1897 Kelly's Directory, was William Buddles who was a joiner and cartwright; secretary was Richard Oram. It was described as having reading, smoking and billiard rooms and a 2,000 book public library established by a Miss Frazer.

However, the original one-storey building was owned in 1873 by a Whitley Bay publican called Mr G.C. Geldard. It was later bought by Simon Henry Frazer who had connections with the Cowpen Coal Company which owned North Seaton Colliery. Other interested parties in that sale included George Downie and Adam Storey. Kelly's 1910 Directory states that another billiard room had been added. The building was of red brick with a stone facing, and had cost £1,900; it seems the library was transferred to another site. In 1914 (probably because of World War One) there were only 151 members, secretary being Fred Dunn.

Plans were released in 1949 to close Newbiggin Colliery and move most of the men to Lynemouth. Probably because Newbiggin was supposedly near closure, at an extraordinary general meeting on 19th December 1959, it was decided to wind up the 'Mechanics Institute Ltd'. Chairman then was Simpson Rutherford Charlton with Frederick Armstrong Mackenzie as secretary. The Institute is seen on left in 1995 during renovation work to Chisholms Bookmakers when Newbiggin herbalist John Imrie painted an elaborate design depicting the Second World War as a celebration of its 50th Anniversary. You will see on right, that 1995 was also the year that extensive alterations were made to Newbiggin's Front and High Street roads and pavements

When the 'Mechanics' building again changed hands in 1965, the 'sureties' of the Institute, as listed on the Deeds of Conveyance were named as S.R. Charlton, Harry Brown, Robert Pringle, James Dickinson, James Taylor, John Arkle, James Booth and F.A. Mackenzie, all of whose occupations was given as either 'miner' or 'retired miner'. The building is now (2002) owned jointly by Newbiggin Sailing Club and Chisholm Bookmakers. The Yard that now houses the Club's boats (seen in photo at a recent Sunday morning training session) was once the vegetable plot for the Old Ship which is adjacent.

In August 1965, work began on demolishing the Newbiggin Colliery Screens, and coals from the pit-head were tipped into railway wagons and transported by tankey to the Screening Plant at Lynemouth Colliery, about three miles away. On 10th November 1967, Newbiggin Colliery ceased to draw coals; and by February of 1968, as the colliery closed, men were either transferred to other collieries or made redundant. Over a period of two years up until 1971, the colliery was completely demolished, the shafts filled in, and the land taken over by Alcan Products of Lynemouth. The land that had been used for the screening plant was taken over by Newbiggin Council and landscaped. The Railway Station was demolished and the land used to build Newbiggin Health Centre. The colliery offices were sold, later to open as a hotel and restaurant called the Minto Lodge (later Hunter's Lodge). As seen in our photo, when the last Newbiggin Colliery miner left he 'hoyed all the tubs off the way'.

Newbiggin Colliery once had its own banner, made of the finest material, and coloured red and gold. It is still to be seen at each Miners' Picnic, even though the colliery closed in 1967. The only problem is that it does not say 'Newbiggin Branch' – it says 'Lynemouth'. This is how it happened. The banner was the brainchild of Charlie Carr who was the Newbiggin NUM branch chairman in the 1950s. It seems he was in the garden one day and picked up a child's drawing which was blowing around in the wind. It showed a boy and girl looking up at the sunrise. This inspired Charlie to copy the drawing as a template for a Newbiggin banner. But when the pit closed in 1967, the miners of Lynemouth Colliery (of whom many were ex-Newbiggin pitmen) cast covetous eyes at their old Newbiggin banner.

In fact, if you look closely next time it is paraded, the words 'Lynemouth Branch' in gold lettering looks a shade lighter than the rest. That is because they cover the original heading. This Bill Harris photo shows the 'Lynemouth' banner at a miners' rally at Blyth, during the 1984/85 Miners' Strike. Two Newbiggin men holding the rope are Thoma Williams and Ray Snell; two others are George Parker and Bob Crooks.

That year-long strike of 1984 was to have dreadful repercussions. It split families, father from son, and acrimony was rife in every pit community. Although Newbiggin Colliery had long been closed, there were still many local men who worked at either Ashington or Ellington collieries. Coal was still being used to heat homes and fuel the cooker – it was a necessity. It was natural that, as the strike began to bite into its second year, miners would look elsewhere for the fuel in outcrop seams. Some men began to excavate down by Siggins Quarry at Newbiggin, with fatal results. Fred Taylor, father of four, was buried under a fall of rock, and died from his injuries. He was yet one more victim.

SECTION SIX

... AND JETSAM

Newbiggin women turned the clock back forty years to commemorate a slice of village history. It was during World War Two that the fisherwomen of Newbiggin helped to launch the Lifeboat in the absence of their menfolk. On 18th June 1984 members of five Women's Institutes pooled their efforts to haul a 12-foot boat nearly a mile from Prospect Place, up Front Street, and along past the Health Centre to the WI Hall in Long Park. They were also part of a campaign involving WI members from all over Northumberland. They carried a banner proclaiming 'Women in the Community' which was to be passed around the county. The photo taken by Bill Harrison shows the group heading towards their HQ.

'People seem to want too much pleasure nowadays.'

So said 91-year-old Mrs Mary Jane Rosser (née Taylor) in the 1950s to a *Morpeth Herald* reporter. 'In Newbiggin, when I arrived in the 1870s, we had time for very little. We had too many stockings to knit and shirts to make for the menfolk. Before the development of the mining industry in Newbiggin, the fishing community was more extensive and more important than it is today (1950s). They also had little time for anything but hard work. I used to see six truck-loads of fish leave Newbiggin Railway Station every day. There was no motor bus, cinema, telephone or radio, only the pleasant clip-clop of horses hooves on the rough unlit roads, with no acrid smell of petrol engines.'

Mary Jane was the mother of Mrs Lambert, wife of Douglas Lambert, once manager of the Midland Bank at Ashington. She was born at Warkworth and came to Newbiggin at the age of fifteen, living there for fifty-five years before moving to Ashington. Her husband was a partner in the firm Rosser and Smith, the contractors responsible for extending the Blyth and Tyne Railway from North Seaton to Newbiggin. Before the opening of this railway extension on 1st March 1872, residents in the Ashington and Newbiggin area had to take the train from North Seaton Station for Blyth and Newcastle. For the convenience of Newbiggin people, a horse-drawn vehicle ran folks between Newbiggin and North Seaton Station (seen here in a George McLean photo in the 1930s). They travelled to Morpeth by the Post Office waggon which left each afternoon.

A happy family group from the 1930s which includes: Grandma Lyle, Florrie Hopper, Lilla Lyle and Ethel Little with her son Derek.

Under the *nom de plume* of 'Wansbeck' (probably the eloquent Alan Robson), the *Morpeth Herald* ran this article in August 1935, extolling the virtues of a trip to Newbiggin by the Sea:

'Newbiggin has been described as "the lung of Ashington" and, as such, is playing an important part these days in contributing to the task of building up a healthy community in a crowded industrial district. Sultry days of July and August have provided Newbiggin with a golden opportunity of substantiating its claims as the health resort, or lung, of a locality whose inhabitants need a way of escape from the grime and fumes of the pit.

'Newbiggin, of course, has its own fumes' problem, but golden summer days, clear skies, clean winds and the blue and green placidity of the sea, have thrust it effectively into the background. What the eye does not see the heart does not grieve over, and the smouldering pitheap and the colliery workings are not visible where the holiday crowds congregate.'

Photo shows a group of Ashington pitmen relaxing on the beach. Second left at back is original Pitman Painter, Oliver Kilbourn, and front left is Frankie Blacklock who emigrated to Australia where he died in 1966.

The Promenade and Beach, Newbiggin 12204

The article continued: 'Observations of the happy holiday crowds that visit Newbiggin these days in search of sunshine, fresh air and freedom, reveals that the beach has, during the summer season, two distinct types of holiday crowds. In the early part of the season, before the commencement of school holidays, the beach scenes are quiet and subdued. The visitors in residence are able to breathe the sea air, bathe and bask in the sunshine in comparative privacy. This is only applicable to weekdays, for the weekend brings the crowds of young workers from the town, young people of both sexes, exuberant because they are free from the restrictive chains of work and labour for a few precious hours. Sunday, especially, is the day of escape. The Sabbath crowds are mainly youthful ... experimenting with the free and frank image of the day and demonstrating their attitude by sun-bathing blatantly before the public eye.

'Young women wear scanty bathing costumes which never have been, and never will be, in contact with sea water. Their limbs are pale and when a gust of  wind blows the stinging sand at them, they shiver and hastily protect themselves with heavy overcoats. Others, more experienced, reveal backs and limbs scorched and blistered by the sun's rays into a condition of painful rawness. They laugh and shout and play, these young people eagerly clutching at life while older folks sit solidly in deckchairs, spectators of the game they themselves once played so ardently in very different circumstances.

'Yes, the beach crowds of today (1935) are different. Many young men are able to display to the world, deeply sun-tanned limbs because modern industry has no need for them. They are the new leisured class, a leisured class without the wealth to enjoy their leisure. Two of them lie face downward on the beach, thrusting their hands into the warm, soft, silken sand. "Aye, Aa was a keen lad in leukin' for work at forst, but Aa divvent care noo," says one. "It's not worthwhile, let's gan for another swim," says the other. Futility and disillusionment ... '

Photo shows Willie Storey with his lifeguard pals and female friends.

'The long day closes and the sun sinks redly behind the houses overlooking the bay. The buses and trains, cars and cycles bear the revellers homeward to put on one more of the chains they so joyously discarded. Deckchairs and tents are stacked away, and the young people who remain grow sentimental. Couples walk slowly along the deserted beach and on the discreetly illuminated promenade. They are young and pleasant to look at. Arms closely entwined, heads together, they walk slowly, the centre of a universe of their own making. They are bent over a sheet of paper. A familiar pungent odour assails the nostrils ... vinegar ... and fish and chips ... even lovers must eat to live, and perhaps there is poetry and romance, even in two fish and a pennorth. Another cameo ... a young man sits on the promenade rail, swinging his feet. His companion, an attractive young girl, is looking up at him: "Aw, you're surely not married, are ye?" she asks appealingly, her tones heavy with disappointment. Another broken romance, another heart temporarily broken. The warning beacons of distant lighthouses wink faintly seaward, and Newbiggin once again becomes a poem penned in moonlight and shadow.

'In August the crowds change in character. The cessation of school lessons releases the hordes of children in Ashington and district from arbitrary time-tables and overworked parents. And they take possession of the beach, their repressed energies finding an outlet in interminable games on the sand, the making of millions of sand-pies and sand-castles, in paddling pools and bathing. There is much shrieking and tumbling, resulting in many

bruises and cuts, the pain and discomfort of which soon disapear in the joy of golden hours of high spirited freedom. (In photo, Willie Richardson Storey on right and his fellow lifeguards were always on hand in case of emergencies.)

'For those parents and children, escaping from the crowded home conditions, the day by the sea usually starts with a bus journey. A small meek-looking man, with his spouse, boards a bus for Newbiggin, accompanied by a noisy, adventurous brood of six. One of the youngters says: "We shud hev had a speshul bus, muther." The parents see the joke and laugh in company with the other occupants of the vehicle.

'At Newbiggin there is a scramble with other equally lively families for space to rest and play. Children are at home at once. It is the one period in the year when the word *Don't* is given a well-earned rest. It is a festival of the family and the willing

The Promenade and Bay, Newbiggin 12419

martyrdom of mothers. Three earnest-looking women with a small harmonium conduct short services on the sand. They tell the unheeding crowds what their hearts are really yearning after. They sing *Tell me the old, old story*, but their hymn suffers from the accompaniment of two down-at-heel cornet players who fill the air with a melancholy ditty *Ole, Faithful pal 'o' mine*.

'Two miners wrangle heatedly about two racehorses: "Aa picked him oot aboot a month ago as a horse to waatch. He ran yistorday, but Aa didn't back him and he won at ten to one." Two others are deeply engrossed in pitwork problems: "So Aa sez tiv the deputy there wud hev to be a change or Aa wud see farther aboot it."

'Said his wife to her neighbour: "Aa canna for the life of me see why Lizzie shud put on such airs and graces just cos she's married tiv a Store grocer. Hor man will not mek haaf as much money as wor Geordie does on coal fillin'." Further on, one man says to another: "There was six on us and

we were aall blind drunk; we had a grand time." And so it goes on all along the congested beach, little people of all ages, bickering, laughing, scoffing, crying. In the promenade bandstand the local amateur orchestra plays: "Oh, I do like to be beside the seaside," and all agree, whether they are happy or not.'

The article concluded: 'In the cool of the evening, tired families trudge to the bus-stands or railway station. The holiday crowds are packed like sardines in buses and trains, accepting discomfort with a smile and a joke. When the last family has gone, the moon and stars contemplate a beach strewn with the untidy wreckage of many beach picnics, torn paper, half-eaten biscuits, and crusts of bread. Another harrassing holiday is ended and Newbiggin once more belongs to its own people. But if the sun shines, the crowds will come tomorrow and the next day and the next.'

For the miners who worked the pits of Ashington, Woodhorn, Linton, Choppington, the Winnin, Barrington etc etc, there was one thought that was predominant in their minds while slaving away in the blackness of the mine – and that was to leave the colliery as quickly as possible to spend some quality time, perhaps with their families, on Newbiggin beach. But Ron Herdman, the *Ashington Advertiser* cartoonist, was pretty near the mark with this 1947 cartoon above showing a filler who couldn't get pit-work out of his mind.

Our anonymous reporter failed to mention the Newbiggin women who helped their fishermen husbands to eke out a meagre living by hawking their fish from door to door. One of these ladies is captured here by Vera Hook's verse and illustration. Vera is a member of Wansbeck Writers' Group:

> I've cod and haddy, ling and
> flatty,
> Fish so fine, fish o' mine.
> Come buy! Come buy!'
> Hear the clear cry.
> A brave and bonny lass she
> stands,
> With glowing health and cheer,
> Braced against the storms of life
> She'll not succumb to fear.
> Her forefathers were fishermen
> Upon the mighty deep.
> Their women-folk were early
> trained
> To do hard work and weep.

The Beach and Pier, Newbiggin 1242

According to the *Ashington Post* Whit Monday on 19th May 1932 was one of Newbiggin's best attended on record as thousands of visitors made the trek either by train, bus or simply on foot. A record crowd from Ashington and district sunned themselves on the beach in the best continental fashion. Trains ran at frequent intervals and small buses carried loads of holidaymakers. The seaside resort was filled from early morning well into the afternoon, swelling the village population to over 30,000. Tennis, golf, bathing and boating were only some of the entertainments which were on offer. From all parts of the north east, many men, woman and chldren came to attend the Faith Healing Mission which Pastor Chilton resumed throughout the day.

In the early 1930s John White, formerly of Beach Terrace now living in Harrow, had this experience:

'I remember the road between the Quay and the White House being very crowded. It may well have been a Bank Holiday Saturday as shops  were open and Manley's and Downie's horses and carts were at the kerb. For some reason, one of the horses took fright and careered into the crowds. One brave chap ran into the path of the crazed horse and flung his arms around its neck. He was dragged along the road for some distance until, with some assistance from others, the animal was eventually brought under control. My lasting memory of this incident was of a group of people trying to calm the horse while others attended to the man of the moment who was standing near the stone structure (in above photo) opposite the White House, obviously very shaken, and with bleeding on various parts of his body.'

In Dr William Stephenson's Health Report for Newbiggin in 1936 it was stated: 'We hope to transfer upwards of 100 families from overcrowded quarters into new houses on the Woodhorn Demesne Estate.' (Note: Photo taken on this 'estate' of Collingwood Road in February 2002 with Woodhorn Colliery Museum, top left, in background.) 'This work is in addition to the provision of 80 houses for those people who had lived in slum conditions. It is proposed to go still further and build another 20 houses between Sandridge and the Church Point for families who could not be removed to Woodhorn on account of their livelihood necessitating that they lived near the sea.' (Note: Attlee Cottages were built in 1938.) The Report continued: 'The nuisance of noxious fumes from the colliery heap has been abated by the construction of a new pyramid heap which replaces the old flat heap. The latter, it is to be hoped, will soon burn itself out. The modernisation of the streets, main roads, etc, is being pushed forward, but I fear that the closet conversion scheme will be delayed a little longer.'

Long John Silver and Jim Hawkins (a travelling youth theatre seen with 1996 Windsor First School children) might well have been looking for buried treasure at Newbiggin in the 1930s, according to the *Newcastle Journal*. The article reported on 'Shepherd's Find of Golden Guineas'.

'Further sensational discoveries are anticipated at Newbiggin. Apart from the antiquarian relics which have already been brought to light at Spital Point, there is believed to be some prospect of Newbiggin's buried treasure being at last located.

'That a considerable amount of money and articles of value are concealed in the neighbourhood is generally acknowledged by the older residents. One of them, Mrs Hall, who is caretaker of the Newbiggin Presbyterian Church, recalled information given to her by her mother, whose death occurred twenty years ago. That story supports local statements that buried treasure does exist, and that part of it, in the form of golden guineas, was discovered about eighty years ago. The discovery of the guineas had been by a local shepherd.

'Whether the recent discoveries on Spital Point of what are believed to be relics of a 14th century leper hospital have any connection with the hidden treasure is a matter of conjecture. It is thought that when the ground on the inside of the hospital foundations is broken, important finds will be made. (Note: 'Spital' is an abbreviation for Hospital.)

'Many of the villagers think that smuggled stores were concealed on the Moor years ago, and practical evidence of this belief has often been given by the 'prospecting' which was attempted unsuccessfully in a secret passage traversing from the sea towards Cresswell.'

Another John White memory: 'The sound of Newbiggin Pit buzzer usually indicated the change of shifts, but was also used to give the correct time of day. The one o'clock buzzer was also a reminder that the school lunch break was at an end and that it was time to get a move on so as not to be late back.

'However, if the buzzer was heard outside of these times, it could easily create panic among families at home, because it was also used to give warning that that an accident had occurred at the mine, and there had been a fatality. It also meant then that the shift was prematurely ended. I would assume that this practice ended with the declaration of the Second World War as the siren then was warning of an imminent air-raid.'

John White provided this photo of the 1939 Newbiggin Salvation Army Young People's Band. That band included a young Nat Graham (seated  bottom left) in its line-up. Nat went on to distinguish himself as a headteacher at Hirst North School and, though retired, he still does stalwart work for the Salvation Army in Newbiggin. Back left: Mrs Major Smith, Alex Humphrey, ?, Fred Humphrey, Alan Graham, Alec Cave, Willie Pattison, Bobby Patton, Major Andrew Smith and John White himself. Seated left: Nat Graham, ?, Andra Smith, Andy Hall, Harry Armstrong, George Graham and Billy Armstrong. Kneeling Len White and ?.

The family of Arrowsmith were well respected in Newbiggin for many years. In January 1939, a valedictory service was held in Newbiggin Presbyterian Church to Miss Nora Arrowsmith who was sailing at the end of that month for Singapore to take up missionary work. The service was conducted by Rev Wallace Kirkby of Newbiggin Presbyterian Church and Rev W. Cullen, minister of St George's Presbyterian Church at Ashington. Two presentations were later made to Miss Arrowsmith (one of four sisters), namely, a cheque, travelling rug, a chair from the church, and a travelling clock from the women of the church. Mrs Dalrymple of Newbiggin, handed over the gifts on behalf of the church, and Mrs Farquhar of Felton, made the presentation for the Missionary Association. Grace Arrowsmith who lived at Windsor Crescent, said of the business: 'We have grown up with the town of Ashington. Much of Station Road in those days was green fields.' Grace and Bessie Arrowsmith are seen in this 1953 Fashion Parade at Arrowsmith's shop. Back left: Margaret Baldry, Grace Arrowsmith, Winnie Barron, Bessie Arrowsmith, Jean Matthews and Joan Green. Front: Elsie Devon, Mary Davison, Mrs Allison and Elsie Clarke.

The Unknown Sailor
by John White

'After a stormy night at Newbiggin, father liked nothing better than to walk along the beach (that is him with white sash, I am to right of three small boys, brother Len on left), or around the Little Bay, to see if anything interesting had been washed ashore. So, clad in mackintosh, wellingtons and a sou'wester, I was taken along too as "the fresh air will do you good". I don't remember coming home with anything important, except for pieces of timber which would "be sure to come in useful".

'It was on a similar occasion in the 1930s when a group of miners met up (maybe they were on nightshift) and wandered around the rocks. Their *find* that day wasn't at all pleasant – it was the body of a man. The corpse was taken to the local mortuary whilst enquiries were made to see if it could be identified as a missing person, or if there had been anyone reported as being washed overboard from a passing vessel. No such reports were received.

'I presume that the local authority then had to arrange a burial, and this was to be similar to a pauper's funeral in some far corner of the churchyard. The Salvation Army at Newbiggin heard of this and volunteered to conduct a service more in keeping with Christian principles. This was obviously agreed as I recall seeing the hearse making its way to the churchyard with a group of people in attendance. Four of the miners who found the man fulfilled the duties of pallbearers. And, yes, you've guessed it ... the four were all

Newbiggin Salvation Army bandsmen. I believe that some kind of headstone was provided with an inscription saying that it marked the last resting place of *An Unknown Sailor.*'

John White's Aunt Muriel who married Jack Woodman, is seen here with this group of Women's Institute ladies in the 1950s. Included are: Rene Jobson, Mrs Dickman, Mrs Alderson, Bessie Arrowsmith, Betty Green, Mrs Gray of Lane End Farm who emigrated to Canada, Mrs Muriel Woodman and Nancy Jones.

When the Second World War got underway, permission was needed from the Admiralty to search at sea. Reports of explosions at sea, sightings of red flares, attending shot-down enemy aircraft are listed in the Lifeboat records. Co-operation with Royal Navy warships, RAF Speedboats and Operation Centres, were all part of Lifeboat activity during the war.

During the early part of the war, a German U-boat sat in Newbiggin Bay, popping off shipping coming out of the Tyne. One such unlucky vessel was carrying Chinese banknotes, made by De La Rue, and millions of cigarettes manufactured by W.D. & H.O. Wills, based on the coast road. That particular ship never got passed Newbiggin, but many Chinese banknotes and cigarettes were washed ashore from the wreck. Young lads thought they were rich as they brought the currency into school, each note showing the face of Chiang Kai-Shek. And miners were in paradise as they smoked the illicit contraband.

The *Eminent* Rescue

Second Coxswain George Taylor took charge of one of the Station's most difficult launches on 4th February 1940. The 'Rescue of the *Eminent*' was put into verse by Albert Morton. Here are a few verses:

> The Belgian boat, the *Eminent*, driven before a gale unspent,
> To be washed up was the captain's fears,
> on those treacherous rocks: the Outer Skeers.
> Although it was a black dark night, Coastguard Harris saw the plight,
> And sent for the Lifeboatmen so brave, these gallant sailors' lives to save
>
> Now Watson's Willie was ill in bed, so Minty coxed the boat instead.
> He said: 'Although the sea is rough, I know my men will do their stuff.'
> They got the boat to the waterside, made a splendid launch on an ebbing tide,
> But alas they bumped the mighty swell that nearly tipped them into Hell.
>
> Then somone said: 'All show your hands, who'll take this boat to the East Sea Sands?'
> They volunteered to a man, so over the Moor the trek began.
>
> They dragged along to different tunes, over the Moor and over the dunes,
> And tried again at a treacherous spot where the water bubbled like a boiling pot.
> The waves were high, the sea was strong, the seconds dragged by, the minutes were long.
> But the crew and boat were stout in heart, and oh, how that sea nearly tore them apart.

(This epic poem goes on for many more verses, telling how the Lifeboat finally prevails against all the odds and saves the eleven crew members of the *Eminent*.) It ends with ...

> Now all you men who sail these shores, please join with me and give applause,
> To the fisher people of this town who did not let your comrades down.

'ALAANG THE NARRA PATH'

When the war ended, a walk to Newbiggin by the Sea became almost a ritual for thousands of Ashington folk. One of the shortest routes, if you lived in the Hirst end of town, was to use the 'narrow path' that began adjacent to the railway line running past Woodhorn Colliery. On our 1930's aerial photo of a sprawling Woodhorn Colliery, loaned by David Brown, you can spot the Narrow Path beyond the coal wagons. That field with hay stacks is now the site of The Churches estate. The pit heap in foreground made way in the 1970s for landscaping the Queen Elizabeth II Country Park and lake.

Here is a recent poem by Ray Wear, dedicated to that route, and hankering after days long gone:

The Narrow Path was always busy
on a sunny summer Sunday,
when pitfolk took their bairns to
the beach
to play in the sand,
and to splash in the Newbiggin sea.

There'd be Newbiggin wives selling
crabs at the gate,
ready to eat, from a catch new in;
cobles at rest, away from the tide,
and whelks you could eat off a pin.

There'd be pit-wives in plodging up
to their knees,
with their skirts tucked up in their
bloomer legs,
and them with mair sense getting
ready for tea,
peeling the hard-boiled eggs.

There'd be seagulls and seaweed,
buckets and spades,
bairns to hap up then set free.
And time to enjoy a penny ice
cream,
on a day by the Newbiggin sea.

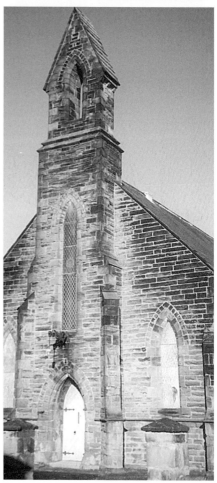

There'd be bells on a Sunday to
ring down the Bay,
with a promise of chapter and
verse.
There'd be pitfolk and fisherfolk
down on their knees
praying life wouldn't get any
worse.

Prayers and promises, fragments of
dreams,
drifting just out of reach.
But it's nice to remember the sand
in your shoes
and the footprints on yesterday's
beach.

For there isn't much left of
yesterday's world,
or the people we used to be;
only that Narrow Path we walked
to Newbiggin by the Sea.

Little Bay, Newbiggin. 11353.

Youngsters arrived at Newbiggin looking for adventure. And there were plenty of places to discover that element of danger, especially if you were a laddie, such as the boys in our top photo, crouched on the rocks contemplating the delights of the Little Bay. Visiting adults and children alike knew they were in for a good time on Newbiggin's wide, sweeping foreshore. The 1930s photo below is taken from the ramp leading down from Beach Terrace and illustrates the panoramic vista that greeted the eyes of people who had got off the bus at Dixon's Corner to descend to the sands at the west end of the beach. It was possible then to plodge about one hundred yards into the sea without it even reaching your knees. Over fifty years of coal extraction by Newbiggin Colliery is blamed for the subsidence that has seen the beach decimated to its present-day level.

The Bay, Newbiggin. 11361.

These were the children still at Newbiggin Secondary School when the war
ended. Back left: Kathleen Bruce, Marjorie Gray, Margaret Pringle, Isobel
Morris, Una Orr, Catherine Hall, Sheila Ross and Joan Blair. Second back: Alan
Brotherton, Michael Corless, Bobby Brooks, Alec Wallace, Jimmy Groves, John
Clavering, Tot Aisbit and Haydn Simpson. Second front: Marion Bullows, Violet
Beal, Molly Storey, Jean Ramm, Betty Smith, Tamar Smith, Sylvia Locker,
Audrey Carr, Heather Barnes and Elsie Smith. Front: Jackie Young, Bobby
Smart, Eric Charlton, Alan Turnbull, Bobby Smith and Bobby Hamilton.

Many of the above youngsters would be caught up in the horrendous winter of
1947 that saw roads blocked whichever way you turned. Newbiggin was
virtually cut off from the rest of civilisation for days on end as six-foot drifts
clogged up the roads right up till March. Our photo, facing towards Newbiggin,
shows that some enterprising council workers had dug a kind of ditch-cum-
path to enable pedestrians to get through. The building in centre is of Mr
Peace's farm while further to the left is the lofty Newbiggin Colliery screens.
New Year's Day 1947 was also a momentous one for Newbiggin miners. That
was the day the pits were nationalised. The red and gold Newbiggin Colliery
banner was unfurled at
the pit-head as the
colliery band played. It
was a big day too for 75-
year-old Charlie Dodds
who was awarded the
British Empire Medal,
handed over by mine
manager Mr W. Stoddart.
Also at the ceremony
was Newbiggin's
youngest pitman that
day, 14-year-old
W. McCarthy.

'That'll Be Ninepence Each, Boys'
written and illustrated by Alan Ross

'Newbiggin! The name, still, conjures up two completely different pictures in my mind. The first is walking back to Lynemouth down the Mill Road on a February evening in a strong Nor'easter after watching my sister (Wor Eva) performing in a play at Newbiggin. It was bitingly cold with flurries of sleet, and I was chilled to the bone. The next day I was diagnosed by Dr Skene as having 'Silent Pneumonia' and whipped off to Ashington Hospital.

'Even now, similar weather rekindles the feelings of long hot summer days, the smell of seaweed and fish, golden sand and ice cream. We at Lynemouth were quite well off regarding beaches; we had 'The Shore' plus Cresswell and Druridge Bay, all three of them had superb sands and dunes, but Newbiggin was special. It not only had good sands with rocks and caves and boats for hire, but also had a promenade, an ice cream emporium, people in droves and a main street with shops.

'Us boys: Brian Wood, Jim Graham, Les Dunning, Ronnie Thomson, Roy Mears, Geordie Cleverly, me and Wor Jim plus others on different days, usually made our way there across the 'Moor' on foot, exploring the caves, cliffs and tanks, and anything of interest *en route*. Our first port of call was always the cliffs under the church to check if there were any coffins bursting from the soil. We were always very disappointed to see the cliffs remained intact. The large cobles drawn up on the beach on their big red wooden-spoked wheels, were our next area of interest, where we paused to admire the lines of the sweeping bows and tumblehome sides plus, of course, the engine, whilst soaking in the pungent fishy, paint and diesel aroma.

'Then it was off to walk along the huge long promenade in bare feet, gazing at the crowds of people having picnics, swimming, playing around in boats

The Promenade, Newbiggin. 10747

(the bay was usually packed with people in boats) riding the ponies on the beach or sampling the Shuggy Boats (remember them?). There was even the remains of a wrecked ship out there on the rocks in the form of two boilers covered with barnacles and seaweed which was a source of great interest and conjecture to us, having been weaned on films of pirate treasure at the local cinemas. We definitely had plans to one day get out there to those boilers for closer inspection.

'Sometimes we walked right along to the Needle's Eye. I once had a drink out of the stream that ran through the Eye, to the horror of my pals, and was scrutinised for days for any signs of poisoning or imminent death. I was a bit worried myself for weeks afterwards. One day I even met Mr Jackson, a Lynemouth School teacher, sailing a canvas canoe, he gave me a short trip along the shore, which was great. I'd never thought of teachers having a life outside the classroom before. Most of us either learnt to swim there, or at least polished up the existing technique.

'But it was the 'Rowing Boats' that was the main attraction for us. There were at least three landing/boarding stages (long slatted wooden platforms with big wagon wheels at one end, pushed partially in to the sea), to facilitate boarding the fleets of rowing boats. These platforms were spaced along the beach, each operated by a fisherman wearing waders, up to his thighs in the water, helping people on and off the boats. We had a go in the boats every visit without fail. But the occasion that I remember only too well was one with Wor Jim (my young brother) and Roy Mears a Lynemouth pal (sadly now deceased). Roy was as keen on boats as I was, so after queuing up and waiting our turn on the stage we eventually got a boat. Roy and I took an oar each, with Jim in the bows, and away we went (we were Dene-trained expert rafters and swimmers). We rowed out, and out, then a little bit further out. I watched the sea colour changing from sandy to green then light blue, and eventually a real dark blue.

'The Newbiggin skyline was a smudge on the horizon, also the motion of the boat had increased considerably. We weren't scared, but decided we were too far out and should get back immediately. Jim wasn't worried about anything, all was well in his world cos Wor Alan would fix it. Well, we headed back and rowed and rowed for what seemed forever but was actually about forty-five minutes until we found ourselves back in the mainstream of rowers. We made our way to the landing stage, having been in the boat for one and a half hours.

'"That'll be ninepence each, boys," said the fisherman as he pulled us into the platform. Roy and I paled and began a frantic search for money. A total of two shillings and thrupence was a king's ransom to us. I had one and thrupence and Roy had ninepence – we didn't have enough. We were in a state of shock – it usually cost us about fourpence each. As a last resort, before owning up, we frisked Wor Jim, and found a very sticky thrupenny bit in his back pocket. Oh, saved, I thought.

Sea Front, Newbiggin.   13679

'That could have been embarrassing or possibly worse. But now we were skint, cleaned out! Mooching along the beach contemplating the changed situation: no Ice Cream, no Shuggy Boats and, even worse, no bus home from Woodhorn Crossroads. Just a long walk with the usual quick peek into *Rammies Ranch*, of course, we couldn't ever miss that. There were many other days out and various incidents after that, but "That'll be ninepence each, boys" became our catchphrase for months afterwards during stressful moments, and it was a huge joke with us. But we were a lot more careful not to go beyond our allotted time in the boats from then on. Aye! Happy Newbiggin Days.'

The year is 1955 and little Lucille Charlton is enjoying herself on the Shuggy Boats in front of the Old Ship Inn. Note the extension to the hotel built on in those days.

I Remember Newbiggin
by Eric Nichol

'In the mid to late fifties I had a contract with the Brown family to transport the fish catch from Newbiggin to North Shields' fish quay. Once a week, occasionally twice, I would have my very first wagon, a Ford Thames, loaded up in the evening with that day's catch. That was then locked away for the night, and at 4.30 am the next morning I would set off to deliver the cargo. Cod, haddock and plaice of all sizes and shapes made it up, and it was conveniently packed in open wooden boxes as in photo, but the smell was always awful and seemed to have a particularly pungent effect on my olfactory senses at that time of the morning. It was not easy to get rid of it either, so my route and the weather often conspired to make the ordeal linger. Darkness and fog combined, frequently necessitated easing up on the gas to avoid taking an unwanted dip in the sea. In those days we were less safety conscious and quayside barriers were a rarity. Added to that was the slow drive past the Tyne Brand factory, where fish paste and fertiliser were made from boiling bones etc. Suddenly the smell of my own cargo did not seem so bad after all.

'Even off-loading the stock was a risky business in those early days. A scratch of the nose, or an adjustment of my hat was quite capable of catching the attention of the auctioneers and have me carrying my cargo back from whence it came.

Auctioning fish at Newbiggin.

Thanks to the diligence of the Brown brothers, Carl and Olaf, that never happened, and I was grateful to them for that, after all, when I got back to Ashington I had coal to deliver, and that was all I could think about.

'They're funny things, memories. Nothing very spectacular ever happened to me on those journeys from Newbiggin to North Shields, and yet they remain quite fresh in my mind. Maybe it was the adventure of travelling along dark deserted roads in the early hours, while sane and normal people remained curled up in their beds. It might have been the curiosity that stirred from glimpsing the practises of another industry, and my utter amazement that its workers could put up with the smell. Perhaps it was that the income from the contract was helping to pay the instalments for my first lorry and vindicating my decision to buy one. I was young then, with energy and ambition. Whatever the reason, I look back with fondness on that time and wonder why it did not seem then as it seems now, and wish, perhaps like all men in retirement, that I had made even more of it.'

Crabs were in short supply in Northumberland in October 1949, but Newbiggin fishermen seem to have been luckier with their catches. One Newbiggin man said: 'Crabs are becoming scarcer every year and if that trend continues in the area then inshore fishing in the area will gradually die out, as crabs and lobsters are the catches on which most of the fishermen rely. Last Tuesday was the first time bad weather have prevented Newbiggin men from going out with their boats, but we were out again yesterday, in spite of the high winds.'

A 1920s fish auction on Newbiggin Beach. Photo loaned by Tom Johnson who owned a number of shoe shops locally; he has money bag and notebook. From left: Mima Perfect, Hunter Brown, ?, Philip Jefferson, ?, Rosie Lansdown, Mary Jane Jefferson (Phil's wife), Matthew Downie, Tom Johnson, ?, ?, ?, Jinny Norman (Luke), Bessie Adams or perhaps Margaret Taylor Armstrong and Frances 'Squeeky' Armstrong (née Lowther).

The *Ashington Post* of 21st May 1950 reported the following: 'The majority of the fish friers in Ashington are members of the National Federation of Fish Friers. The twenty-one Ashington members have been unofficially recommended to maintain prices at the old level. The standard fish supper costs 11d, including eight pennyworth of fish. The Newbiggin fish sales depend largely on the catches brought in from other ports, especially at North Shields. Good catches at North Shields give local buyers a chance of cheaper fish at Newbiggin. A good average catch of a Newbiggin boat is 40 stone, and, on Tuesday, a late arrival brought in 60 stone of good fish.'

BEM for Adam Storey

In the 1951 Honours List, the Grand Old Man of Newbiggin, Adam Storey, was awarded the British Empire Medal for his services as inshore fisherman and Lifeboatman. Unfortunately, he died one week before the award at the age of ninety-eight. Adam was a familiar and colouful figure on this particular part of the Northumbrian coast. He had been in the Lifeboat crew for thirty-nine years and received a Lifeboatman's Certificate in 1932.

In February 1951, Newbiggin Urban District Council applied to the Ministry of Health for £6,326 to provide Newbiggin with a full electric street lighting system. It was in order to start the first section which comprised the Newbiggin Colliery area, Woodhorn Lane (in photo below) and Front Street, moving towards Spital Farm. The village was then partly lit by electricity, but the majority of streets, plus the promenade, were illuminated by gas standards. The new scheme provided for 240 lamps of various types and power that would bring the total of electrically lit lamps in Newbiggin to 288. Three large lamps that were erected at the Railway Station, the West End and the White House were allowed to stay lit all night, but the remainder were extinguished at 10 pm.

Our photo of a Millennium parade shows that the corner is now under surveillance from a security camera attached to the White House on right.

'Make Coronation Quiet, say Newbiggin Councillors' was the headline in the *Morpeth Herald* of 10th October 1952. The Coronation of Queen Elizabeth II was treated as a low-key event by some members of Newbiggin Council. Chairman John Adams pointed out that at the last Coronation (King George VI) the council had spent the equivalent of a one penny rate. He said: 'We should be very careful what we do in this matter. I feel that the state of the country is so fixed that this is one time a Coronation should be very quiet.'

He was supported by Cllr Edward Willis who warned that they should be careful in what they do, especially as it may turn out to be 'wasteful'. Cllr Mrs Eastlake urged her colleagues to do something in the way of giving the public a lead, while Cllr Jack Smith supported her view, stating that other local councils were already considering plans.

While the councillors were bickering, Newbiggin folks were making their own preparations, and many street committees were formed to organise street parties and to present the youngsters with Coronation mugs to commemorate the event.

In 1950, the Newbiggin Church School was situated down Simonside Terrace; for many years Mr Hollingsworth was head with Miss Dawson and Miss Armstrong as teachers. This group attended in 1950. Back left: John Lowery Bobby Armstrong, George Robinson, Barry Turnbull, Ronnie Robinson, Bob Humphrey, John Huddlestone-Brown, Jimmy Brown, Hennor Rowe, Billy Beers and Alan Peel. Middle: Mary Keys, Marie Corless, Kathleen Nisbet, Brenda Lampton, Joan Crozier, Ella Turner, Ann Wake, Agnes Fairbairn, Margaret Edgar and Mark Denton. Front: Jannie Nichol, Ivy Clarke, Margaret Hancock, Jean Hayworth, Mrs Dawson, Eizabeth Moffatt, Ann Young, Annie Davison and Joyce Davison.

Councillor Jack Mather was head at the Colliery School in 1950. He is seen here with back left: Jimmy Ingham, John Sands, Brian Strachan, John Sampson, Terence Armstrong, Leslie Wills, Alan Wilkinson, Ken Armstrong, Ray Armstrong, Leo King, Michael Bell and John Martin. Middle: Alfie Wallace, Michael Turner, Robin McMahon, Tommy Lowerson, Ann Redfearn, Alice McMurdo, Irene Dunn, Joan Peel, Richard Renner, Jimmy Rogerson and Billy Taylor. Front: Christine Sampson, Doreen Holdroyd, Pauline Messenger, Ann Ashurst, Isobel Storey, Mr Mather, Joan Davidson, Agnes Beatty, Patricia Wake, Margaret Wallace and Doreen Nichols.

Miss Ivy Whitelaw took charge of the Newbiggin Presbyterian Church Choir in 1952 when a play, produced by her father William, was performed in the Church Hall. This was followed by the Choir, represented by young choristers who included: Eric Dodds, Louise, Nancy and Pearl Dixon, Alan Armstrong, Connell Charlton, Jeannette Smith, Elizabeth Morton, Alice Green, Joan Simpson, Margaret Neil, Bobby Hyde, Jackie Johnson, Pamela Ruddock, Billy Gray, John Mason, Carol Dixon and Laura Tunstall. Keith Swailes is 4th left in front row wearing hat.

Newbiggin Scouts had a treat in 1951 when they travelled to London to take part in the Festival of Britain celebrations. Kneeling in front are Garth Dance, George Willis, Derek Palmer, Colin Long, Willie Patterson, Ivan McDonald and his brother, Alan Thompson, Tom Hyde, Ken Covell, Maurice Lynn, Reed, Maurice Priestley and Billy Brown. Those standing at back include: Norman Lowery, Joe Horn, Norman Elliott, Ken Wake, Mr McDonald, Aubrey Devitt, Eddie Fenwick, Bob Dickman, Ted Dixon, MP Will Owen, Billy Dance, Ken Spowatt, Stan Carr, Alan Thorn, Jim Hedley, Ben Hyde, David McPhail, Tom Swailes, John Sands, Billy Maughan and Fred Clennell.

The 2nd Newbiggin Scouts Troop paraded behind the Mothers' Union Cottage in the early 1950s and the group included at back: Brian Redfearn, Andy Groves, John Burton, Leslie Wills, Bill Brown, Tommy Cassidy, Eric Mountford, Michael Donelly. Those in centre include: Jack and young Vera Wills, Les Atkinson, David Burton, Peter Marshall, 'Butcher' Richardson. In front, among others, are: Alan Lowery, Mrs Highmoor, the vicar, Jimmy Highmoor, Eddie Adey, Jack Dodds and Gordon Highmoor.

Miss Norah G. Brown took on a new role when she produced a play performed by the Newbiggin and Woodhorn Women's Institute Drama Club in May 1952. It was an experimental play that the group had previously performed at the Drama League Festival in Gateshead. Members of the cast of *While there is Time* were Elsie Hindle, Lilia Main, Elizabeth Dickman, Irene Robinson, Lorna Clark and May Alderson. A second play entitled *The Vixen and the Grapes* included some of the above, joined by Betty Carter and Elizabeth Hedley. Stage lighting effects were carried out by Jim Victor Hughes. This is the Women's Institute pantomime Cinderella from 1972. Back left: Betty Carter, Janice Spowart, Doris Chape, Amy Firmin, Doreen Oliver, Jill Reid and Pat Hindmarsh.

In 1952, the NCB's proposals to take a railway near the ancient village of Woodhorn were strongly opposed by the Vicar of Woodhorn, the Rev Archie Davison, and the councillors of Newbiggin. Despite being situated on the main road with plenty of traffic, Woodhorn Village retained a lot of its 'old-world' atmosphere, and the vicar maintained that this would be spoilt if the Coal Board was allowed to put a mineral railway line to the east of the village, between Woodhorn and Newbiggin.

It was planned that this railway would link up Lynemouth and Woodhorn collieries as part of the surface development scheme of the NCB. The railway would carry coals from Lynemouth and Ellington pits, estimated to be in the region of 19,000 tons a day. The railway would cross the road between Newbiggin and Woodhorn by means of a bridge, swing right near the railway line and cross the road again near Woodhorn Bridge. Above is the bridge as it now stands near Woodhorn Church. The vicar said: 'It would be a crime to ruin one of the loveliest little villages in the north east. Let us hope that the Coal Board will amend its scheme.' Newbiggin councillors had suggested that the railway be taken north of Woodhorn, going underneath the road, north of Woodhorn Mill, by means of a tunnel.

Railway enthusiast John Talbot from Oxford explains a little more:

'This particular part of the railway eventually opened in 1956. It is downhill all the way at a gradient of 1 in 150 from Woodhorn to the concrete bridge north of the Spine Road roundabout. Then it is 1 in 284 to the next bridge over the road near Woodhorn Church; and 1 in 132 from there to Lynemouth.

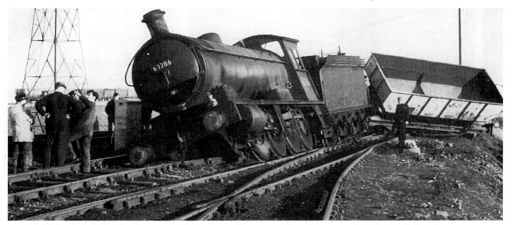

'With hindsight, this was a bit steep for some trains and inevitably there was a big crash (as seen in Peter Robinson's photo above). This engine weighed a massive 110 tons and had steam-operated brakes on all its eight wheels, and on its coal-tender's six wheels. Despite that, it was unable to hold back the momentum of its train of 30 coal wagons coming down the hill. The wagons propelled the engine into derailment, and piled up behind.'

Newbiggin Church School was tucked away around Simonside Terrace. In 1950 these pupils attended. Back left: John Lisle Robinson, John Armstrong, Billy Warrender, Roy Denton, Billy Brown, Brian Edgar, Robert Wilson and Bob Crozier. Middle row: Gordon Gray, Ken Miller, Marjorie Renner, Audrey Weatherall, Stan Thornton, Richard Robinson, Jimmy Summers and Terry Turnbull. Front: Isabel Beers, Margaret Booth, Joan Merryweather, Veronica Gordon, teacher (unfortunately her name is unknown), Audrey Hancock, Joan Alexander, Joyce Armstrong and Rita Fairbairn.

Miss Ivy Whitelaw was always keen for her pupils to enjoy the spoken word and in 1952 she coached this group of Secondary School pupils to compete in the Choric Speech competition at Newcastle's City Hall. Back row left: Maurice Priestly, John Hughes, Brian Clark and Jackie Johnson. Middle: Michael Conway, Adele and Eileen Storey, Irene Maclean, Malcolm Lindsay. Front: Monica Turnbull, Susan Ditchburn, Pauline Northcote, Sylvia Wilkinson, Shirley Hedley, Miss Whitelaw, Ruth Nesbitt, Eileen Priest, Janet Milburn, Thelma Boaden and Margaret Elliott.

In 1954, Newbiggin Lifeguards were awarded the Chronicle Cup for the most efficient life-saving team. Working hand-in-hand with the lifeboat, the 20-strong life-savers, consisted mainly of miners, trained by local coastguards, Michael Dobson and Bill Tallman. Number One in the team was 56-year-old underground bricklayer, Jack Dawson of 6 Holly Avenue, Newbiggin. Before him, his father John was connected with the team for nearly forty years. No 3 in the team then was Tom Dawson, a jobbing builder, of Collingwood Road. He is the brother of Jack, and another brother, George, was also a member of the team. Seen in this early 1950s photo, the Lifeguards include: Bill Snell, Jackie Fail, Denton Snell, Tom and George Dawson, Wilf Armstrong, Ken Thornton, Philip Miller, Twizel Cookson, Jonna Brown, Mr Campbell, Johnny Storey, Ted Martin, Jimmy Wallace and Jack Dawson

Lisle 'Ernie' Willis was a well-known Newbiggin character. A teacher at Hirst Park Modern School, he became a Newbiggin councillor in 1949. Educated at Morpeth Grammar School, Ernie, who lived at number 3 Beach Terrace, served with the RAF during World War Two. He was keenly interested in amateur stage work, and applied his talent in assisting with stage productions at Hirst Park Boys School in Ashington.

Ernie, whose father Edward was also a Newbiggin councillor, was at one time prospective Labour candidate for the Berwick Division, but withdrew his nomination in January 1954 because of 'pressure of work'. He had written many plays, and wanted to concentrate on screenwriting – he was already one of the writers for the Tyneside radio show, *Bob's Your Uncle* and TV's *Ned's Shed*. His son Simon Willis was also involved with local BBC Television as a presenter in the 1980s, and now works for the BBC in Glasgow.

Malcolm Mackenzie in Australia remembers that when he lived at 65 Meldon Terrace for a while, he frequented a barbers, and Ernie Willis used the same establishment, often entertaining customers as they waited. He also recalls that Mrs Willis ran a baby-wear shop further along the street. Malcolm's niece worked at Newbiggin Library in the 1950s at the same time as novelist John Braine who was lodging then with a family called Ormandy. Malcolm also says we can't compile a book about Newbiggin without mentioning zany character Hector Mackinnon of 'Hector's Snack Bar' fame.

So here is Hector appearing on Newbiggin Bandstand around 1938. Hector's party piece was playing the harmonica. Nothing out of the ordinary there. Ah, yes, but Hector played it with his nose! Other musicians from back left: George Rosemorgan, Wilf Peel, Billy Robson. Centre: Dick Shepherd, Hector MacKinnon, Joe Llewelyn, Bob Spence. In front: Ernie Guthrie the drummer.

Eva Adey (now Mrs Birch) said of her uncle Hector: 'I worked for him when I left school at fourteen. I didn't mind the job, but I was only paid ten shillings a week, and that was from 8.30 am until nine at night. Some nights he would let me go to the pictures, but I had to go back to work when the pictures came out. We got a lot of soldiers in the Snack Bar for cups of tea. I remember that Hector gave me one shilling for my Christmas box.'

Newbiggin had its share of characters, both male and female. Such as Freeholder, Miss Ann Mann, seen in her coffee shop in 1960.

Newbiggin's Co-operative Dramatic Society performed on Tuesday 20th March 1956 at the Co-operative Hall. The chosen play was a farce entitled *Queen Elizabeth Slept Here*. As usual, Matt Gibson was the producer and Ivy Whitelaw played one of the leading parts. What made this play special was the appearance of John Braine, local Newbiggin librarian then, who was to go on to write a major novel called *Room at the Top*, later made into a film. According to an *Ashington Post* review: 'Undoubtedly, William Dent stole the show and Ivy Whitelaw as his wife produced a very good display. A special mention must be made of 13-year-old John Turnbull who had only four reheasals before taking the stage. The set was excellently done and praise is due to Will Denton and carpenters J. Lawson and R. Armstrong; the decor by Bob Cessford and lighting effects by J. Victor Hughes.' The cast was as follows: Robert Mills, Ivy Whitelaw, William Dent, Joy Warne, Gordon Booker, Hannah Hughes, Sally Hedley, James Batey, Margaret Taylor, Pat Stafford, Alan Anderson, John Braine and Edwin Davison. Actors in photo from left are Bill Dent, Ivy Whitelaw, Pat Stafford, ?, Jim Batey, John Braine and Joy Warne.

Many party nights were held by the Newbiggin Co-operative Players, and here we have a happy crowd from the mid-1950s. Leaders of the pack from the front are: Lottie Harrison, Peggy Punton, Ena Deans, Matt Gibson, Ivy Whitelaw, and then a selection of Mr and Mrs Billy Thompson, Bobby and Mona Mills, Margaret Elliott, Vida Sample, Bobby Ferrel, Bobby Richardson, Edwin Davison, Charlie and Iris Watson, Isabella Simpson, Vic and Hannah Hughes, Hilda Oliver, Billy and Anna Dent, Sally Hedley and Jenny Gowland.

Newbiggin Secondary Modern School Choir was voted top of the pops in 1952 when they won an award at the Wansbeck Music Festival. The golden voices belonged to back left: Elsie Dickman, Rhoda Bye, Eileen Davison, Pat Lowery, Margaret Friberg, June Curry, Jean Bell, Jacqueline Simpson, Ann Scott, Audrey Hankins and Jean Pringle. Second back row: Brian Redfearn, Dennis Todd, Hazel Robinson, Brenda Lord, Pat Storey, ?, Pat Connell, Margaret Winter, Margaret Lord, Doris Bullows, Yvonne Atkinson, Derek Armstrong, and Andy Doyle. Second front row: Miss Swann music teacher, Dorothy Brotherton, Elizabeth Smith, Betty Mason, June Chesterson, Sheila Ross, Olga ?, Rosalene Callan, Margaret Rutter, Katherine Reay, Joyce Armstrong, ?, Joan Thompson, Frances Priest and Mr Hargreaves music and art teacher. Front row: Thomas Hyde, Arthur Clough, Don Hamilton, Reed Rowell, Lawrence Coutts, Garth and Derek Dance, Derek Lucas and Tommy Casson.

Verification came in February 1963 that work was to go ahead to straighten and rebuild the road near North Seaton Hall on the route to Newbiggin to eliminate a 'dangerous curve'. The total cost was to be nearly £20,000 with the aid of sixty per cent by the Ministry of Transport. The North Seaton Road where the improvement was to take place had 'been a danger spot' for some years through the re-building work around the former Hall grounds. The site was to be used 'for a model housing project'. North Seaton Hall was another of the region's 'treasures' that was demolished in the cause of 'progress'. In its time the Hall had been home to landed gentry and coalowners. William Watson who owned most of the land in that area was the first occupant. In the 1930s it was a holiday home for deprived Tyneside children. German prisoners of war were camped in the grounds in the 1940s. And Newbiggin Council acquired it after the Second World War for families waiting to be re-housed. Following complaints of woodworm in the building, the 'easy option' was taken and Newbiggin Council agreed to its demolition.

It was all change in 1963 for 600 children from Lynemouth, North Seaton and Newbiggin with the building of a new Newbiggin County Secondary School at a cost of £295,000, covering a site of just over 18 acres. The head of what had been the 'Modern' school, Mr Billy Bell, moved across as the new head. Meanwhile, back at the Infants School in Cleveland, Miss Peggy Punton and Miss Doreen Wedderburn had to take both their classes over to what then became Newbiggin County Modern Junior School.

Photo includes: John Straker, Alan Robinson, N. Milne, Geoff Hudson, Gordon Scott, John Ramm, Steven Foster, Ross Atkinson, Alan Harold, John Neil, Ken Hedley, David Bowie, Peggy Punton, John Rees, Alec Graham, Michael Peek, Linda Cookson, Vivien Hall, Lorraine Sanderson, Romayne Taylor, Helen Robinson, John Corney, Chris Lynn, James Armstrong, Ian Buller, Miss Wedderburn, John Gray, Glen Telford, Lynne Miller, Joan Waldock, Linda Reed, Margaret Neil, Linda Warham, Joan Burt, Anne Young, Chistine Henery, Mary Linda Hope, Glynis Bell, Vivien Tenwick, Alan Armstrong, Keith Wilson, Stuart Downie, Pat Park, Susan Carr, Christine Johnston, Susan Kay, Helen Robinson, June and Cora Gilchrist, Sheila Sill, Glynis Peek, Jean Perfect, Ann Armstrong, John Downie, Hector Galley, John Imrie, Bob Chilton, Terry Wilson, Yvonne Jacques, Ina Bennett, Eva Bennett, Ann Hopper, Pauline Jobson, Vivien Furness, Mary Hindhaugh, Judith Oliver, Carol Murray, John Elliott, Stephen Rowe and Edward Groves.

During World War Two, the beaches around Newbiggin had been sealed off for defence purposes. At the end of those six years, many tons of sea coal lay scattered after being washed ashore by the tides. It was said that you could step straight off the cliff on to a pile of coal. Sometimes as many as a hundred horses and carts worked on the beaches around Lynemouth. The supply of coal showed no signs of abating as Lynemouth Colliery put in a speedy tipping belt in the early 1950s to tip even more waste into the sea. A smaller version of this belt can be seen on the left in our photo. Lynemouth residents bemoaned the loss of their beloved Strawberry Hill as it disappeared under the belt's foundations.

'Time is running out for the sea coal pickers.' That was the headline in the *Ashington Advertiser* in May 1963. A new stone-screening plant at Lynemouth Colliery, which  was expected to come into operation in June, was estimated to save about 33,000 tons of coal a year, but it meant the death of another 'coal industry' on the area's beaches. This meant that virtually no coal was to be tipped out to sea, but was to be pumped out as waste. This had a serious effect on the sea-coal industry which provided a living for men from Newbiggin and Lynemouth (as seen in photo) and also the loss of cheap coal for householders. Sea coal, once described as 'big business' by some people, almost came to a full stop as much of the easy pickings, previously garnered from local beaches, had come from Lynemouth tip. From that date, all colliery waste was to be pumped out to sea as crushed stone without a particle of coal. The paper went on to say that 'perhaps the golden beaches of Lyneburn, Cresswell and Newbiggin may some day return'.

One of the longest service launches for the Newbiggin Lifeboat occurred on 4th September 1964, as reported in the *Newcastle Evening Chronicle*:

'A Lifeboat (*Richard Ashley* – seen below) groped its way though thick North Sea fog to safety last night. Women wept when the Newbiggin mercy craft edged cautiously to the beach after 19 hours at sea. A boy whimpered in his mother's arms: "I want my Daddy. He's been away a long time." Sight of the vessel ended many hours of worry which started with a radio message from the crew: "We don't know where we are." The Lifeboat from Newbiggin was one of the vessels searching for a mystery boat which sent a distress call ... one of the crew, Cllr Dennis Taylor, said: "We had a nasty time coming in and we owe a lot to HMS *Surbiton* (the fishery protection vessel) who at one point took us on board and gave us food and cigarettes." Cliff Hancox, the mechanic, said he did not have any trouble during most of the day, but there was difficulty in making for the home Station in the fog and darkness. "We switched off the engines after asking for assistance and we heard a sound which gave us guidance." As he hurried home for a meal, 47-year-old George Miller Dent of Bay View West said: "It was just another job, only longer than usual ... "'

Newbiggin has had its fair share of tragedy and grief, as Richard Martin's *History of the Lifeboat* will testify. But time has distanced many of the 19th century events so that they appear to have taken place in a different time warp, leaving present residents unaffected by them. However, there are still many living in Newbiggin by the Sea who can remember all too clearly the events and emotions that were laid bare on the evening of 4th August 1966.

Richard Robinson and his father and mother watched TV that night. As usual, his brother Bill was at the first-house pictures at an Ashington cinema, coming out at eight o'clock so as to be back in time for an all-night stint at sea. At half past eight Ned Robinson followed his evening ritual of going outside to see what the weather was like. The sea was calm, and about an hour later Ned Robinson and his two sons Richard and Bill, launched their coble, the *Eventide*. Waving goodbye to them from their home perched high above the beach at No 1 Bay View East, Tamar Robinson had done this a thousand-and-one times, yet always mindful that she might never see her loved ones again. That night her worst fears were to be realised.

Ned Robinson had been thirty years old when he married local Newbiggin girl, Tamar Armstrong, having met her at the Chapel. Ned's grandfather was the famous Billy the Whaler. Tamar's honeymoon was barely over when she was introduced to that least favourite Newbiggin women's chore: baiting the fishing lines. By watching Ned's mother and sister at their seemingly endless task, which began at 4 am, Tamar soon became skilled and, between them, the three women baited over 2,000 hooks with mussels in preparation for a single trip.

Tamar bore her husband three sons in five years: Bill, Richard and Ronnie who took the trade of colliery electrician in preference to being a fisherman. Edward 'Ned' Robinson is seen centre with Richard on left and William. In 1963, Ned paid £1,400 for what was his third boat, the *Eventide*. A year later it was involved in an incident with a Polish trawler when the large vessel ran into the coble's nets and dragged it for half a mile before the net could be cut free. A lucky escape. Not so lucky was that night in August 1966 when the *Eventide* ended up on the bottom of the North Sea, nearly three miles from shore. It was a mystery. Reports that a Polish vessel was in the vicinity, and may have snagged its nets were never verified. Three lifeboats from Newbiggin, Blyth and Amble were later joined by the Tynemouth lifeboat, plus HMS *Belton* and the sea-fisheries vessel, *Northumbria*.

That night, foreign ships were anchored close inshore, sheltering from bad weather in Alnmouth Bay. Only one vessel lay at anchor in Druridge Bay – the

scene of the tragedy. In photo right, the *Harvest Queen* from Seahouses, crewed by two brothers, Raymond and Douglas Rutter, manages to raise the *Eventide* from the bottom of the sea, but there was no sign of its crew.

NEWBIGGIN DATES (FACES AND PLACES)

Records show that the first St Batholomew's Fayre and Market began in the early years of the 13th century. And it was another bright day for the 1999 Fayre Day, seen above. Regular market stallholders, the Newbiggin Women's Institute, on this occasion were represented by: on left Lorna Clark and Amy Firmin, while Gladys Henderson, Betty Carter and Jill Reed get a day off.

1220 - Approximate date for building of St Barthlomew's Church.

1235 - Newbiggin Freeholders claim rights from this date.

1352 - Indulgence of 40 days granted to Newbiggin folk to 'repair and maintain pier'.

1733 - Newbiggin policeman's duties include: 'to taste all ales sold in town'.

1796 - Soldiers 'encamped' on Newbiggin Moor under Lt Colonel Dalrymple.

1838 - Freeholders grant land for building a 'Presbyterian Place and Sunday School'.

1843 - William Dent defies Freeholders and builds a house on Common land.

1851 - Newbiggin Lifeboat in action for the first time.

1851 - Newbiggin is listed as 'a chapelry and village' with a population of 717.

PRESBYTERIAN CHURCH AND COUNCIL SCHOOLS - NEWBIGGIN.

St Mark's Presbyterian Church (above) was built in 1868.

1870 - Local Government Act adopted in Newbiggin; council elected later.

1870 - Newbiggin lit by gas obtained from a limited company.

1872 - Branch railway line linked North Seaton and Newbiggin Station via Ashington.

1876 - Wesleyan Methodist Chapel built, costing £1,420.

1884 - Church of England School opened down Simonside.

1885 - Newbiggin Golf Club formed, another, the 'Eastcliffe', followed soon after.

1891 - Newbiggin Institute founded, with reading, smoking and billiard rooms.

1894 - Newbiggin constituted as an Urban District Council with seven members.

1900 - Swimming Races take place off Newbiggin beach.

1901 - Miners from North Seaton buy 'The Elders' for a workingmen's club.

1902 - Plans drawn up for a 'tramway' between North Seaton Station and Newbiggin.

In 1904 three suspected cases of Smallpox were treated in Newbiggin, one in Brewery Yard which is to the rear of building in photo. This was the 'park' prior to becoming the 'Memorial Park' (at one time it had been a pond). Signpost points: 'To the Old Ship Inn – First Class Accommodation for Visitors – Lunches, Dinners, Wines and Spirits – Good Stables.'

1904 - Seven Newbiggin men perish trying to aid the steamship *Anglia*.

1908 - New Dolphin pub was rebuilt with J. Graham as manager.

1909 - Arthur Peebles awarded bravery medal for attempted rescue in Newbiggin Pit shaft.

1910 - First sewer laid by G. Edgar and Jack Rutherford, blasted track over to Church Point.

1910 - First coals drawn at Newbiggin Colliery.

1910 - Central Club opened with officials, J. McDowell (secretary) and Dave Gibbons (chairman).

1911 - Pipes laid for fresh water into Newbiggin houses.

1911 - W. Warbeck, first man killed at Newbiggin Colliery.

1911 - Miners bought larger premises for their club, called the 'Bank House'.

1912 - During a national miners' strike, a soup kitchen was set up in 'Dolphin Tea Rooms'.

1914 - Another version of Mechanics' Institute built (one-storey building).

1914 - Store Arcade built with T. Welsh an official.

1915 - Baden Powell in Newbiggin to present medal to Jack Grant for saving a boy scout.

1916 - George Blair of Allison's Yard, one of 13 men killed in Woodhorn Pit explosion.

1919 - Ivy Leaf Club opened (beside Windsor Gardens), closed in 1943.

1920 - Appearing at Empire Cinema, Newbiggin, silent film, *Edison* about the inventor.

Colliery Street & Monument, Newbiggin. 5059

It is a safe bet that one of the only men to own a car in Newbiggin in the early 1920s was the travelling photographer who took these two photos. On above – he has obviously parked his car next to the War Memorial and wandered up Woodhorn Road to find the best vantage point to take a picture that would encompass the newly-built colliery houses, the Memorial and the Colliery School in the distance.

Windsor Road, Newbiggin. 5609

And here we have what looks like the identical vehicle – registration BB 892 – parked outside the newsagent's shop in Windsor Road, probably on the same sunny day. Again, our intrepid cameraman has retreated to the end of the road so that he could get a photo that would include the shop (to sell his postcards once they were printed) and the top of the Horsehoe Steps leading to the sea. That shop was later called 'Crackets' and is now a B & B establishment.

During the 1926 Miners' Stoppage, soup kitchens were set up in the Queen Vic and local chapels. This particular group who helped out at one kitchen look more like entrants in a fancy dress parade. From right: ?, ?, ?, Jack Dixon, Norman Buddles with ham bone, ?, Harriet Chilton, Jack Adams, Miss Skeldon and Billy Brown. Kneeling Dickie Allison.

1929 - First part of New Prom was built from below Beach Terrace to Bank House.

1929 - County Modern School opened at Dixon's Corner.

1930 - Empire Cinema changes to Wallaw, named after new owner Walter Lawson.

1931 - Mainly because of immigrant miners, Newbiggin's population now stood at 5,761.

1932 - Major fire at Newbiggin Co-operative Store.

1932 - Hospital on 'top of Moor' destroyed by fire.

1936 - First (and only) Northumberland Miners' Picnic held at Newbiggin – it rained.

1937 - In February, the fishermen's huts beside the Lifeboat House were pulled down.

1938 - Bertorelli's Cafe opened on Easter Monday.

1941 - Six Newbiggin residents killed on 7th November by German bomber.

1944 - Some 205 children attended County Modern School of whom 14 were evacuees.

1946 - Ladies (members' wives) were admitted to Central Club for first time.

1946 - James Wood, new head of County Modern School, formerly at Nedderton School.

1946 - 8th June was day of Victory Celebrations. Newbiggin childen received a florin (10p).

1946 - A girls' netball team was formed at Newbiggin County Modern School.

1948 - Swimming lessons began on beach for pupils of County Modern School.

1949 - Mr J.W. Armstrong was given permission to sell whelks on Newbiggin beach.

1949 - Draughts competitions held on large-size, open air board, near the bandstand.

1949 - North Seaton Colliery Band play Sunday concerts in August on bandstand.

By December 1949, the *Ashington Advertiser* was reporting Newbiggin residents' fears about the closure of the pit. It stated: 'As the flow of men to Lynemouth from the doomed pit at Newbiggin continues, people in both communities are hoping that the planners will not let the need for coal dominate everything else in the district. One is that Newbiggin does not become a 'dead town', as so often happens when the local pit closes down. At the present moment it is considered that the men transferred from Newbiggin to Lynemouth will continue to live in their home town, and no definite plans have been made for an extension of Lynemouth Village.

'If these plans by the NCB remain unaltered, say local people, Newbiggin and Lynemouth can benefit if the problem of increased waste from Lynemouth Pit (seen above in the 1950s) can be solved satisfactorily. The old scattered colliery workings at Newbiggin can be eliminated, together with the pit heaps. If railways have to be built between Newbiggin and Lynemouth, residents hope that they will be screened and not transformed into goods yards. With improvement to Newbiggin, it could be linked up with Lynemouth's sea front. People do not want the area transformed into a gaudy, money-making resort, but developed on a modest basis which could offer healthy and useful amenities, not only to them, but to much of mid-Northumberland.'

This 1950 netball squad played at the Secondary School. Back left: Mrs Hetherington, Patsy Wallace, Margaret Robinson and Miss ?. Front: Beryl, Violet Beadle, Edwina Armstrong, Sylvia Locker and Marion Bullows.

This 1952 team played there two years later. Back left: Olive Brown, Joyce Maughan, Mrs Telford, Frances Priest and Dorothy Brotherton. Front: Joyce Parmley, Margaret Rutter and Pat Lowery.

The Colliery School in 1950. Back left: Leonard Lansbury, Arnold McDonald, John Lindsay, John Robinson, Alan Simm, Bob Hartley, Dave Emery, George Bell, Chris Armstrong, Billy Gray, Bob Hodgetts and Bob Armstrong. Centre: John Courtney, Albert Hudspeth, Jack Hindhaugh, Ivy Robinson, Ann Highmoor, Brenda Scott, Carol Ford, Rita Lindsay, ?, Gloria Friberg, ?, Douglas Hunt and Miss Hall. Front: Anna Turner, Carol Turnbull, Ida Dunn, Ann Turner, Barbara Mead, Valerie Bell, Ann Ingham, Audrey Potts, Sandra Horwood and ? Holdroyd.

1951 - School dinners commenced at Colliery School, cost 7d (3p) per day.
1951 - New canteen for school dinners built at County Modern School, Miss Stokes, cook.
1951 - Britain's oldest pitman, 81-year-old Fred Ruddock, finally retired at Newbiggin Pit.
1952 - A big surprise at local election was the success of Jack Smith as an Independent.
1953 - Workmen's Golf Club, the 'Eastcliffe' ceased to function.
1954 - W. Twizell & Sons landed 140 stones of skate in one catch.

Jack Ramm was awarded lease for caravan site at Church Point for £500 in 1957. It is now perilously close to falling into the sea, as can be seen from this 2002 photo.

And one more netball team in 1957. Back left: Anna Turner, Brenda Stock, Miss Ann Carrick and Jean Pyle. Front: Jean Earl, Margaret Booth, Ann Highmoor, Rita Lindsay and Audrey Potts.

Secondary School's 1958 Senior football team. Back left: John Twizell, Peter White, Jimmy Younger, Dick Robinson, Ken Miller and John Telfer. Front: Mr Smailes, Ken Haggerty, Ronnie Freeman, John Lindsay, Dave Emery, Rob Armstrong and John Taylor.

This was the 1958 Junior football squad. Back left: Alan Redden, D. Williams, Gareth Wood, Ronnie Parmley, George Thornton and Mr Graham. Front: Derek Peart, Brian Price, John Pattison, Ken Dunn, Michael Gale, Rodney Foster and Tommy Patterson.

In 1959/60 this was the girls' netball team that represented Newbiggin County Modern. Back left: May Brown, Miss Ann Carrick and Norma Wooten. Front: Edwina Martin, Maureen Miller, Vivien Scott, Shirley Atkinson and Betty Warrender.

Heavy sea damage to Newbiggin sea front was cause for concern in June 1966 when promenade railings were pounded to pieces, leaving no barrier between the prom and the beach below. Newbiggin councillors feared that someone could fall from the 175-yard stretch that had been left unprotected. When heavy seas rolled on to the sea front earlier that year, heavy logs in the boiling surf smashed down the cast-iron railings. 'Someone could break a leg there,' warned Cllr George Nesbit. 'What if there was a high sea and a child came along and fell into the sea?' Council Surveyor, Hector Galley, said: 'It will be two months before the replacement railings are delivered ... the only alternative is to erect warning signs on the promenade or close it completely until the new fencing is ready.'

It was in 1972 that Newbiggin Women's Institute celebrated their 50th anniversary. The WI ladies have always been held in high esteem by the local community. They are seen at their presentation of a garden seat to the people of Newbiggin, to be placed near the Health Centre. Seated at the front are Lorna Clark (president) and councillors Geoff Spain, Annie Hepple, Elizabeth Eastlake and one un-named. Lady WI members from back left include Doreen Oliver, Jean Dunn, Peggy Hindmarsh, Mrs Horn, Mrs Young, Mary Henderson, Mrs Robson, Hilda Thornton, May Alderson, Mary Brown, Betty Carter, Mrs Mills, Kitty Johnson, Mrs Lilburn, May Robinson, Nell Lewis, Mrs McKie, Mrs Jed Brown, Ivy Seely, Etta Lewis and Mrs Foreman.

The 1st Newbiggin Girls Brigade Band, who met in St Andrew's Methodist Church, taken in Simonside in the 1970s. In those days the band master was Jackie Summers who also had his own danceband. Girls from back left: Veronica Thompson, Diane Graham, Karen Lowther, Carrianne Sampson, Jayne Hartley, Janet Graham, Gail Brown, Glynis Aspin, Angela Mills, Clair Emery and Tracey Gould. Front row: Dawn Saunders, Michelle Hudspith, Lorraine Dean, Nicola Weeks and Michelle Fogg.

The year of 1974 was a turning point in many ways. No longer would small communities have their own choice of a local school. It was a system not widely welcomed by some teaching staff. The new system decreed that Newbiggin secondary pupils would be taught at Hirst High School which had just opened the year before with Mr Richard Houlden as head. These four modern misses were affected by  the move many years later. Newbiggin girls, Amy Liddell, Elizabeth Imrie, Claire Wilson and Laura Knight, are seen soon after receiving their GCSE results in 2001 at Hirst High School.

What had been Newbiggin Secondary School now became a Middle School for 9-13-year-olds. Newbiggin's original secondary school at Dixon's Corner became Newbiggin West Junior School as long-serving teachers were uprooted and posted to vast  impersonal comprehensives. Photo shows headteacher Mrs Eleanor Hunter, seated, with school secretary Jennie Richardson and five young pupils at the old 'Cleveland School' in the early 1970s.

More than a century of service by Newbiggin fisherwomen was recognised when a tribute to these women was included in the annual Lifeboat Harbour Day on Saturday 5th August 1978. Ladies of the Newbiggin Lifeboat Committee recalled past years by dressing in traditional fisherwomen garments of black skirt, white aprons and black shawls as they served the many customers attending the various stalls. Ladies from back standing left: Etta Lennox, Mrs Whitcombe, Mrs Brown, Nancy Storey, Blanche Armstrong, Mary Humphrey, Lily Charlton and Edna Storey. Front left: Sally Robinson, Alice Newman, Mary Hall, Sheila Train, Grace Patton, Mrs Detchon, Sylvia Bennett, Alice Gilligan, Lily White, Nan Graham, Betty Clive and Mary Robinson.

And these were some of the original Newbiggin lady collectors that the above were emulating.

'No Other Business' was the last call on 26th March 1974 when Newbiggin Council found itself amalgamating with its near neighbours, Ashington and Bedlington. In an emotional evening, Cllr Geoff Spain said: 'I like to think everything we have done has been in the interests of the public at large. One thing no-one can take away from Newbiggin councillors past and present is that we have tried our best. The local authority had 468 houses before the second war, but we have built 1,325 post-war houses. Our first factory came in 1971 and the second in 1973, but I hope it will not be long before we have many more.'

Vice Chair Mrs Elizabeth Eastlake replied: 'This is a momentous day. In some ways it is a sad one because I think, for the size of Newbiggin authority, it has made wonderful progress. When you get among bigger authorities and see what they have done then Newbiggin does come out on top. We have not only made progress, but have a tremendous community spirit. Newbiggin has been big enough to do big things and yet small enough for us all to join together.' She later paid tribute to the 'late Mrs Annie Hepple', who became the first woman councillor in Newbiggin.

Elizabeth Eastlake.

Newbiggin Golf Club officially opened its new £46,000 clubhouse in July 1974, two and a half years after the old wooden building was destroyed. The plush new clubhouse was opened by club president George Bilton. When the old building, which had stood since 1920, was destroyed at New Year 1972, the club appointed a committee of 'leaders' to plan and launch the fundraising efforts for the new clubhouse.

Since then every member played his/her part to raise the £12,000 which the club had to provide. Grants of £2,500 each were received from the Sports Council and the Playing Fields Association, while Vaux Breweries financed the scheme to the tune of a massive £26,000. The club captain, Michael Porter, said: 'We have an excellent stewardess in Mrs Jean Dower, for whom residential accommodation is included in the building. Tom Fairbairn has taken over fully as the club professional. We have three greenkeepers and they are looked over by the experienced eye of Ron Downie, chairman of the greens committee.'

The clubhouse photo was taken in February 2002.

The Promenade, Newbiggin. 13766

There have been a vast number of changes to Newbiggin sea front since the 'new' promenade was opened in 1932. Sitting outside the Old Ship Hotel was a regular occasion then for the many men who had retired or were simply waiting to go on shift at the colliery – as in our photo above. You can still find men gathered in little clusters on the prom of 2002, but it may not be so tranquil as in bygone days as they huddle behind the huge sea wall that blocks out their view of dwindling sands. It is true that the prom nowadays boasts inlaid tiles of pink, yellow and beige, but it isn't used exclusively for 'promenading' any more. In the mid-1990s an experiment began to allow cyclists on to Newbiggin prom for the first time and a cycle route was laid that joined Newbiggin with Woodhorn Colliery Museum and beyond. On the opening day a cycle rally was held and all who completed the course were awarded a medal and certificate, as seen on photo.

This is the staff that began at what became Newbiggin West Junior School in 1974. Back left: Miss I. Lang who lived at Stakeford, Miss Susan Howey of Morpeth, Brian Todd of Ellington, Miss Frances Holmes of Seaton Hirst and Mrs Brotherton (school secretary) who was from Newbiggin. Front left: Mrs Sally Dawson of Newbiggin, Miss Peggy Punton (who provided photos) of Newbiggin, Mr G.K. Scott (head) from Gosforth, Mrs Margaret Straker of Newbiggin and Mrs Win Noble.

Deputy Head Peggy Punton had this class in 1974. Back left: Peggy Punton, P. Harrogate, Gary Norris, Paul Scott, Michael Bye, Andrew Knox, Edward Lowery, Brian Smethan and student teacher Miss Butler. Middle row: David Peart, Wayne Gibson, Paul Laws, David Rowell, Diane Elliott, Karen Linsley, Stephen Ralph, Roy Thompson, Nicholas Johnston and John Dunn. Front row: Beverley Scott, Helen Alderton, Suzanne Morris, Michelle McClusky, Elaine Price, Kimberley Steele, Susan Hudspeth, Sharron Brown and Sharron Storey.

In January 1978, residents of Newbiggin were up in arms over the dilapidated condition of part of their town. For the past two years the residents of Simonside Terrace had been complaining to the local authority about the view from the rear of their homes which overlooks a 'rubbish dump'. They also complained about the road at the back of Simonside which 'has an old-fashioned cobbled surface full of holes, which is too narrow for cars to manoeuvre in'.

'Many cars get so far up the lane then have to go back,' said one of the residents, Mrs Doris Thompson. 'This must be the only street in Newbiggin that has not been modernised by the Council, and surely it is one of the most deserving,' she said. Mrs Yvonne Lowther, who had lived in Simonside for 19 years, said: 'Old fireplaces, mattresses and all sorts of other rubbish is dumped here. The weeds grow waist-high in the summer and there must be a high risk of disease with so many flies collecting there in the warm weather.' Cllr Joe Caine, chairman of Wansbeck environment services committee, said: 'The job of improving the road is being held up because of difficulties over some land needed for the work to be carried out.'

A TRIBUTE TO

Jackie Milburn
TYNESIDE'S FAVOURITE SON

"This video will be a rare tribute to one of the immortals of the game whose fame carried far beyond the soccer field. He stirred passions on the terraces, thrilled millions with his skills and left everyone with a genuine sense of loss at his death.

VIDEO GEMS

Note: As a postscript to the above story, in 1989, I was involved with Tyne Tees Television as the writer of a documentary about the life of footballing legend, Jackie Milburn. The director wanted to show a young Jackie, played by 10-year-old Jeff Dillon, kicking a stone on a cobbled back street – but none was to be found in Ashington!

I suddenly remembered the back lane of Simonside, so the camera crew flocked to Newbiggin for the day. So if you happen to be watching the video *JET – A Tribute to Jackie Milburn*, supposedly kicking a stone in an Ashington back street – that was Simonside!

The photo left shows Jeff kicking a stone, followed down Simonside by cameraman Dave Dixon and sound engineer Ed Wood.

Two young Newbiggin-trained boxers were in the limelight in April 1977 thanks to Newbiggin Sports Centre boxing coach, Terry Coulson, who said: 'I have the best two kids at their respective weights in the North of England. They are so good that I have trouble arranging fights for them now.' The two lads Terry was praising were 14-year-old Michael Mason and Michael Shutt, aged twelve. Mike Mason, on left, who lived in Allen Road, Newbiggin, and attended Hirst High School, represented England Schools against Wales, and boxed for North-East Counties on six occasions. Young Michael Shutt then lived in Beverley Gardens, Stakeford, where he was a student at Guide Post Middle

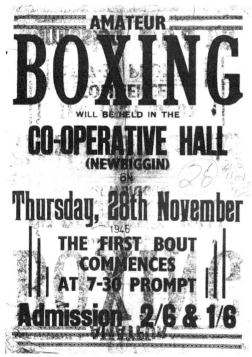

Newbiggin always had a boxing tradition that is still carried on by the highly successful Dolphin Boxing Club. This 1946 poster shows bouts took place in the Co-operative Hall, top entrance price being half a dollar.

School. Weighing in at only four stones nine pounds, he was reigning North East Schoolboy Champion in 1977. That same year Mike Mason won the National Junior ABA Championship at 51 kilos, and was voted Wansbeck Young Sportsman of the Year. He turned professional in 1980 and won his first ten contests as a featherweight. Now forty years of age, Mike is involved in runnng his own boxing gym at Craghead, county Durham. He said: 'I have four good lads in training, two of whom are National Champions. My son Mick is also a successful boxer – he will be twenty-one next year. I never lost touch with Terry Coulson – he is now my father-in-law!' Michael Shutt, living at Stakeford, retired from boxing when he was eighteen years old, having added the County ABA Light Flyweight title to his list of successes. He now works for a housing co-operative.

There has been no shortage of celebrities willing to turn out at Newbiggin for various functions, most of them have their price! Of late we have had pop stars Leo Sayer and Showaddywaddy entertaining the crowds at the annual fair. In 1995 it was the turn of Jack Charlton to officially open Northumbria Water's new sewerage plant. As he stood addressing the crowd he joked: 'Aa thought they were kiddin' when they said I was to stand in front of the 'piazza'. Aa thought he was an Italian striker!'

It was the turn of another footballing celebrity, Malcolm Macdonald, to declare open the 1998 Lifeboat Day. Pity that he began by saying: 'I would like to thank the people of Newbiggin on the Sea for inviting me.' SuperMac is seen making friends with young Adam Kirkup.

There was another Newcastle United connection in 1993 when Magpie Charlie Crowe from the victorious 1951 FA Cup-winning team made an award of school equipment, paid out of the Jackie Milburn Trust Fund, to Windsor First School. On left is head, Lorna Cunningham and, on right, teacher Marilyn Mullaney. The £300 award bought material for the Special Needs department. Royalties from Charlie's latest publication the *Newcastle United Scrapbook*, published by The Peoples' History, continues to be used to help deprived north-east children in need.

Hundreds of loyal local supporters and guests gathered for the opening and dedication of the refurbished Lifeboat House on 12th June 1999. The Station still uses the original Boathouse, built in October 1851, and is the oldest operational Boathouse in the British Isles. Proceedings were opened by Stan Green, secretary, with Andrew Ashton, Divisional Inspector of Lifeboats, handing over the Boathouse to the Newbiggin Branch. Jack Smith, former secretary, unveiled a commemorative plaque and cut a tape (see photo) to officially open the Boathouse. A large buffet prepared by the Ladies' Guild was set out in the Boathouse and a commemorative cake, donated by Donkin's Bakery, was cut by Jack Smith to complete the day.

I took this photo of some fresh-faced youngsters enjoying a morning playtime at Moorside First School in March 2002. Probably some of them took part in the dedication of the *Monocap* beside St Bartholomew's Church in Millennium year. Then they would have joined children from Windsor First and Newbiggin Middle School in singing one of my songs:

'Newbiggin, Newbiggin, Newbiggin by the Sea/take a trip on a sailing ship and soon you will agree/that everyone enjoys it, from one to ninety-three/at Newbiggin, Newbiggin, Newbiggin by the Sea. You'll forget your boring tellies when you get to Bertorellis/and who can paint a better view than that at St Bartholomew. Down at Newbiggin, Newbiggin, Newbiggin by ... give it a try ... Newbiggin by the Sea.'

The People's History

To receive a catalogue of our latest titles – send a large SAE to:

**The People's History Ltd
Suite 1, Byron House
Seaham Grange Business Park
Seaham, County Durham
SR7 0PY**

www.thepeopleshistory.com